おもろすぎるわ日本人!

どーもどーもパラダイス

ファン・ボルガ著

"Domo Domo" Paradise

Fun Volga

> I love Japan!
> This book is filled with my funny and unforgettable culture-gap experiences in Japan.
> If you want to make friends with foreigners in Japan, this is a must-read!

Fun Volga

©2003 Text by Fun Volga
©2003 Illustrations by Kazunori Hosoma

はじめに

English Zone編集部

「この本だったら、ぜんぶ英語だけれど何とか読めそう…」そう思って、この本を手にしてくださった皆さん、どうもありがとうございます。その選択は正解です！

中級以上をめざすあなたの英語メディア、「English Zone」（奇数月1日発行）が自信を持ってお届けするEnglish Zone Books第一弾！ それが本書「どーもどーもパラダイス」です。

この本は、遠くアルゼンチン出身で、英語をベースに国際的に活躍しているファン・ボルガさんが、日本での生活の中で体験したカルチャー・ギャップ体験を、おもしろおかしく、しかもやさしい英語で書いたユーモア・エッセイ集です。

最初は一年だけの予定で留学生として初来日したボルガさんですが、結局、日本の会社に就職して気がつけば在日10年以上に…！ ラテン系のテンションの高さと早合点しがちな性格も手伝ってさまざまなハプニングを繰り広げるのですが、どれもこれもとにかくおかしくて、思わず笑いがこみ上げてきます。ボルガさんからの読者のみなさんへのメッセージ「A Final Word」（170ページ）まで、とにかく笑わせてくれます。

また、この本の一番の特徴は、語彙的にも表現的にもやさしい英語で書かれている、ということです。高校生までに学習する単語を中心に書かれています。それ以外の単語や、教科書にあまり出てこない口語的な表現は、巻末に注釈をつけています。

「英語の本を辞書なしで読めて、しかも笑える！」このエッセイ集は、あなたをユーモアの世界に誘ってくれるはず。この1冊を読み終わったら、もうあなたは次の英語の本を探していることでしょう！

Let's have a laugh together!

すいせんの言葉

「ある、ある、同じカルチャーギャップ体験！」

ダニエル・カール

　まずこの本の原稿を読んで思ったのは「ある、ある、同じ経験！」ということでした。日本に住んだことのある外国人なら、多かれ少なかれ経験するだろうカルチャー・ギャップをボルガさんは、おもしろおかしく書いてますね。

　この本のタイトルにもなっている「どーも」、これくらい外国人にとって不可解な言葉はありません。短くて聞き取りやすい言葉だからかもしれないけれど、日本に来たばかりのころは日本人の話す言葉の半分くらいが「どーも」に聞こえたことがあります。僕はもう日本に22年間住んでいますが「どーも」の持つたくさんの意味を理解して、使い方がきちんとできるようになるまで10年くらいかかりましたから。

　逆に何年たっても慣れないのが満員電車。定員の何倍も乗っているギュウギュウ詰めの満員電車は違法ではないか、って真剣に思います。一度体調の悪いときに満員電車に乗って、内臓を圧迫されて気絶したことがあります。

　「外国人は日本語ができない」という日本人の先入観も確かにあると思います。山形駅で「酒田行きの電車は何番線ですか？」って、後ろ向いている駅員さんに尋ねたら「３番線です」。ところが振り返った瞬間に「ナンバー・スリー！」。

　こんなような出来事は日本に住む外国人は誰もが体験していることだと思うけれど、ボルガさんは楽観的な人ですね。日本の社会を自分の価値観や考えで判断しない。批判もしない。自分の勘違いなどのミスを素直に認めて、カルチャー・ギャップも最終的

には現実のものとして受け入れている。だから長年日本に住めたのでしょう。

　外国に住む、ということはある意味で、外国語を勉強するのと同じことだと思います。新しいことに挑戦する、わからないことがあっても失敗してもあきらめてはダメ、繰り返し慣れていくことが大切です。

　このエッセイ集は文章全体が会話的でありながら、ちゃんとした文章になっているので、繰り返して読むのに最適です。日本の英語教育は読み書き中心で日本人を悩ませるような、頭を使わせるような勉強方法がまだまだ多いでしょう。ボルガさんのストーリーは、とにかく軽快なテンポで書かれているから、そのノリで読み進んでいける。英語の勉強になるだけでなく、国籍を越えた、お互いの理解のためにも、この１冊はきっと役立つと信じています。

Contents

はじめに 3
English Zone編集部

すいせんの言葉 4
ダニエル・カール

"Domo Domo" Paradise 9
便利で不便？ 多すぎる「どーも」の意味

To Eat, or Not to Eat 19
日本食が苦手だとどうなるの？

Talk to Me, Please 29
日本語を覚えたい外国人共通の悩みは？

Renting a Piece of Tokyo 37
異国日本での夢の一人暮らしの第一歩！

Train Shock 47
地獄の通勤ラッシュをやり過ごすには？

Sweet Melodies of Love 55
セレナーデを歌うラテン式求愛の成果は？

Osaka in White 61
日本では結婚披露宴まで儀式みたい？

Meetings and More Meetings 73
退屈な会議を楽しく過ごす方法とは？

Who Cares? …. 81
ビジネスでのカルチャー・ギャップはもっときつい？!

International Business …. 89
海外出張でハプニングに見舞われる！

A Dog in My Life …. 97
犬は飼い主に忠誠を尽くすのではなかったの？

Lines into the Future …. 105
占いにばかり頼ってはいられません！

Night Hunter …. 111
リサイクルよりエコロジカル？ 粗大ゴミの再利用！

OL Ways …. 119
すごすぎる存在感、OLは社内最強の味方か敵か？

Surviving at the Office …. 125
日本の会社で生き残るための処世術！

Red in the Face ···· 131
日本人女性好みのルックスに挑戦！

A Perfect Salad ···· 137
日本語を話せるのは日本人だけではありません！

The Fortune of My Love ···· 143
占いに自分の恋愛を賭けられる？

巻末注釈 ···· 151
役立つ単語・イディオム集

おわりに ···· 170
著者ファン・ボルガさんからのメッセージ

"Domo Domo" Paradise

便利で不便？ 多すぎる 「どーも」の意味

初来日した、まったく日本語がわからないボルガさんの耳に、
やたら飛び込んできたのが「どーも」という言葉。
それがお礼を言うときや礼儀正しく振舞うときに使う言葉だと知り、
初対面の人に「どーも、どーも」と言ってみると、相手はニコニコ。
これは便利な言葉だ！と思ったけれど、次第に
その言葉の持つ意味の多さに混乱するようになって…

At last I was in Japan. I stepped out of the plane into the Narita Airport building for the first time. I was walking towards immigration when I saw it. It was the first time in my life. Two Japanese were standing in front of each other, bowing, bowing, and bowing. The greeting seemed to last forever. There was something else though—something very shocking. They were saying many things, but I could not understand. For the first time, I was in a country where I could not even guess a single word of the local language. To me, whatever those two guys were saying to each other, it just sounded like noise. However, I could pick up one of the sounds very clearly. It was *DOMO*.

「どーも」は "Thank you" だと教わったけれど…

On the way out of the airport, I could hear again and again that same *domo*. I had to find out what it was. Walking right beside me was a French businessman on his second two-day trip to Japan. He looked like an expert on things Japanese. "Well," he said, "my experience has taught me that it means something like thank you." He went on explaining. "Whenever you want to thank anyone for anything and be polite at the same time, just say '*domo*' and it will be all right. And don't forget: You have to bow every time you say thank you." On hearing that I said to myself, "Hey, this is a very handy expression. I must remember it."

When I arrived at the dormitory, a professor from the university was waiting for me. I wanted to make a good impression. So I bowed and said something like "bla bla bla *domo* bla bla *domo domo domo*." I took great care to say the *domo* very clearly. The rest was in a very soft and impossible-to-understand voice. Just the sounds.

Notice that I repeated the last *domo* three times. I wanted to sound very polite. In English it would sound very strange repeating thank you, thank you, thank you, so many times, but in Japanese it did not sound bad at all. Anyway, I didn't know what I was saying. The professor looked at me and smiled. "Oh! You speak Japanese very well." I was very happy. Only a few hours in the country and I was already mastering the rules of being polite in Japanese.

Later the same day, I met another professor. I bowed and again said the same unrecognizable sounds and the clear *domos*. It worked well. This professor, too, smiled and congratulated me for the outstanding Japanese I could speak. The French businessman was right. A bow and a *domo* and everybody is happy.

One of the guys from the dormitory broke my tennis racket. He could not speak English very well so he said something like, "*Domo*, racket no good." He seemed to be very sorry. But he was saying *domo*—thank you. I got kind of angry! You can imagine. I lend him my racket, he breaks it and comes back saying, "Thank you." Unbelievable! Anyway, the following day he bought me a new one.

The other day I was outside the dormitory waiting for Yoshitaka to pick me up. He was quite late, in fact more than 30 minutes late. Aren't the Japanese usually on time? Perhaps my friend was different. At last he turned up. "*Domo, domo*. Did you wait long?" He came at me waving his right hand. "These Japanese are really funny people," I told myself. "He is late and comes saying, 'Thank you, thank you.'" I was getting very confused. In this country do you have to say thank you for everything you do?

とりあえず会話の最初に、いつも「どーも」と言ってみることに

I had already been in the country for four months and I still could not speak Japanese. But I wanted to sound as polite as possible. Therefore, I began to speak very strange-sounding English. Here are some examples:

"Thank you, I was late."

"Thank you, he seems to be quite crazy."

"Thank you, this rain doesn't seem to stop."

"Thank you, excuse me."

"Thank you, I thought I saw Mr. Tanaka, but it was another person."

"Thank you, he doesn't seem to understand."

"Thank you, it has been a long time since we met."

"Thank you, thank you."

Everybody seemed to be very pleased when talking to me. "You are getting to be very Japanese," they used to tell me while smiling. Well, I thought, in English it sounds strange to me. However, it is very close to the way people speak here. So, I kept talking that way for quite a while.

発音しやすいけれど、難しかった「どーも」の使い方

After seven months, my Japanese had not improved. In fact I didn't study the language at all. But I had became very good at saying, "Thank you." I had also made lots of friends. One evening I was standing with one of them, Koji, at the south exit of Shinjuku Station. We were supposed to meet his girlfriend and go drinking. She was a little late. We were talking about women always being late when, suddenly, a guy came running from nowhere without looking. He ran into my friend. The crash knocked poor Koji to the floor. Koji looked very angry. The guy stopped and said, "*Domo domo*...bla bla." I could not understand the rest, but I think it was something like, "Thank you, thank you. I wasn't looking." Koji didn't look angry anymore. He stood up and said something in Japanese. The other guy bowed two or three times and left.

This is a very happy country, I thought. Even if someone is very angry, no one ever fights. Just say, "Thank you" and everything is solved. It reminded me of

Carnival time in Rio de Janeiro, Brazil. There, too, everybody is happy. Even if you get angry, the noise and the music make you forget about it very soon. Here, in Japan, that music seemed to be "Thank you."

I explained my ideas about *domo* to Koji. He could not stop laughing. At last he said, "There are many different *domos*. One for each occasion. Indeed, it seldom means thank you." I discovered the great mistake I had been making. The *domos* I translated as "Thank you" weren't always the same *domo*. Most people must have thought that I was a very strange person, saying, "Thank you" whenever I opened my mouth.

数年後、「どーも」を使いこなす達人に！

Many years have passed. Although my Japanese is still far from perfect, I became a professional at *domo*-ing. I found it to be a very happy expression.

Not long ago, I was packing my bags to go back home for a vacation. Suddenly the doorbell rang. My friend James was there. He had been in Japan for only one month and was planning to stay another two years. He was carrying a box with him. He asked me, "Could you please give this little present to my girlfriend when you arrive?" He said "little," but to me the box looked very big. I took a quick look at my bags. They were really full and very heavy. It was impossible to make anything else fit in. However, I felt kind of rude saying no. Without even thinking about it, my face changed into an expression of worry. I said, "*Sore wa doomo*..." James looked at me very surprised and asked, "Why are you thanking me? This is not a present for you." I was too tired to explain anything, so I gave him a copy of this article.

To Eat, or Not to Eat

日本食が苦手だと どうなるの？

日本に来たばかりのころは、日本食が大の苦手だったボルガさん。
海苔は不気味だし、コンニャクはゴムみたいだし、
味噌汁は熱すぎるし、白いご飯は味がない！
貧乏留学生だったボルガさんは、
ハンバーガーやカップラーメンで急場をしのいでいました。
見かねた友人が日本の伝統料理を、と
ある店に連れていってくれましたが…

I always remember with great pleasure the days when I was a student at Sophia University. Life was most interesting. Not only did I have to study very hard, but also, I had the difficult task of eating every day. Now, you might be wondering what is so difficult about eating every day. Let me explain myself better. Please read on.

悩みは日本食嫌いで、さらにお金がないこと

First of all, I was on a very tight budget. In other words, I had very little money. Besides, I did not have much time to do part-time jobs because the university kept me very busy. As a result, I could not afford to go to nice French or Italian restaurants. Anything with a price higher than 700 yen was not on my list of possible choices.

"What is your problem?" my friends used to ask. "There are many restaurants where you can eat good Japanese food for 700 yen." That was true, but I didn't like Japanese food.

To tell you the truth, I hated it. I could not stand the sight of *nori* (seaweed). White rice was completely tasteless. I would have to ask the waiter to put some butter or mayonnaise on it. *Miso* soup was always too hot; sometimes it would even have some little pieces of something that tasted like rubber in it. People tried to convince me that it was something very good for my health called *konnyaku*.

Please note that now, after quite a long stay in this country, I have gotten very used to Japanese food. A day is not complete for me if I do not have at least four or five cups of green tea. Anyway, going back to the main subject, I had a big problem when I first arrived. Burgers and fried potatoes saved me for a while. But not for long. I got tired of them very soon. Can you imagine? Burgers for breakfast. Burgers for lunch. Burgers for dinner. I even used to have dreams in which the burgers would run after me.

安い洋食、カップヌードルを食べ続けたら…

One day a friend told me he had "the perfect solution" for me. He handed me "cup noodles." They were just the right food for me. It was love at first sight. They did not taste very good, but for 120 yen I could make a little extra effort. However, my "noodle life" did not last long. After one month of eating only noodles, three times a day, I had lost almost 10 kilos. All the girls I knew wanted to know what my secret was. I never told them the truth. Someday I should write the *Fun Volga Diet Book*.

The taste of food was not the only problem. The Japanese language was another big headache. Before coming to Japan, I had been told that most Japanese could understand English.

However, that was not the case at most of the restaurants I used to go to. Because my Japanese wasn't very good, the form of communication we used had to be very simple—body language plus some simple Japanese words.

I used to make the guys working at the restaurant come out with me, and then as I pointed to something in the window that looked delicious, I would say: "I want to eat *kore*."

The waiter would reply, speaking very fast: "*Tonkatsu desu ka?*"

Me: "No! I don't want to eat 'cats'. I want *kore*!"

Waiter: "*Tonkatsu desu ne!*"

Me: "No! No cats!"

At that stage of the conversation, I was sure that the delicious looking dish in the window by the door of the restaurant was CAT. So the only thing I could think of to do was to leave in a hurry with a clear and loud "*SAYONARA*," and go to the next restaurant. The conversations with the waiter in the place where I used to eat went something like this: "I want to eat this."

"This?"

"Yes, yes—this."

"OK. Please come in and sit down."

Sometimes, it was not so simple, and I had to run many times from the table to the window, taking different guys with me each time. Once, I even picked another customer by mistake. There were very special occasions when friends invited me to dinner. Most times they let me choose the restaurant. My choice would always be a steak house.

But other times they would make the choice. I remember once when Yoshitaka invited me out. He decided to take me to a traditional Japanese restaurant.

魚の生造りには驚き！

"You have to try different things," he said. We went to one of those restaurants with an aquarium or fish tank very close to the door. The door opened, and one of the guys inside, all dressed in white with an army-style haircut (very short), shouted something like *rasshai* (welcome, come in). We were shown to a table and sat down. The place was not very crowded and was very clean. A man sitting at a table next to us caught my attention. He was having some real problems trying to catch with his chopsticks the pieces of food that were jumping around on his plate. Then the waiter came with two nets! One for me and one for Yoshitaka.

What would the nets be for? Are there mosquitoes in this place? I wondered. It was a mystery. The waiter showed us to the little aquarium. Yoshitaka was very experienced. He looked for a while and very soon made a choice. The fish tried to jump out of the net, but could not escape. Very soon it became sushi. Now it was my turn. Yoshitaka had gone back to the table. I was left alone with the waiter.

"Choose one," he told me. I looked more carefully, and this little gray fish caught my attention. At first, I did not like the idea of seeing my dinner swimming one moment and on my plate the next. But, I thought, this meal is free, and I have to gain as much experience as possible while I am in Japan. It did look delicious. So nice. It got closer to the glass and started to look at me. I tried to catch it with the net, but it managed to escape the first time, and the second. The waiter was clapping his hands beside me. "Once more, once more. Try a bigger one." The little gray fish was still looking at me. Those eyes seemed to say, "Please don't eat me."

When I went back to the table, my friend Yoshitaka asked if I had already ordered. "Yes!" I answered. His dinner arrived first. On my friend's plate, little slices of meat were still moving, and at times they seemed to jump from one corner to another.

"I like fresh fish," he said and began to eat happily. Then the waiter came with my order: soup, two eggs, and a bowl of white rice.

"Are you sure this is what you want?" Yoshitaka asked, a bit surprised.

"Yes! I feel like eating only this," I said, while drinking the soup and pouring mayonnaise on the rice.

Yoshitaka was very surprised when it was time to leave, because the waiter brought me the little gray fish swimming happily in a not-so-little plastic bag.

I could not stand the thought of someone else eating it. Now he still swims very nicely in a small aquarium in my room. His name is Mac.

Talk to Me, Please

日本語を覚えたい
外国人共通の悩みは?

外国語を学ぶなら、
その言葉が日常的に話されている国に行くのが一番! とよく言われますね。
ボルガさんもそう思っていましたが、
日本は果たして日本語を学ぶのに一番いい国なのでしょうか?
日本語がなかなか上達しないのはなぜ?
そんなボルガさんが見つけた最高の日本語の先生とは?

Wise people say that if you want to learn English, you should go to Britain, the U.S.A., or some other English-speaking country. Similarly, if you want to study Spanish, then the best place to go is a country where Spanish is used in everyday life, like Spain or Mexico. How about studying Japanese? I'm sure your advice would be, "Go to Japan!" But wait a minute. Are you sure Japan is the best place to learn Japanese?

As you may know, I didn't even think of studying Japanese when I came to Japan. I really didn't need it. Wherever I went, there was someone who could speak English. The conversations weren't great, but we communicated. People I met on the street wanted to use their English. Drunks would say to me in broken

English, "Here, we speak English. Go drinking together." I often refused those kinds of invitations. During the daytime it was the same. "May I practice English with you?" OLs used to ask me in the train. I never said no. People in Tokyo are very friendly, I told myself many times.

After some time had passed, I decided to study Japanese. That's when the problems began. I wanted to practice but everybody kept speaking to me in English. Could they all have forgotten Japanese? I wondered.

日本語を話したい外国人共通の悩み

"Hey, no one wants to speak to me in Japanese!" I told Terry, a Canadian studying at Sophia University. "It's the same with me," he replied. We asked other foreigners. They all had the same problem. What could we do? We decided to practice among ourselves. "From this day on, we will speak to each other only in Japanese." With those words, we started a Japanese-speaking club at the university.

However, our conversations were very simple. "*Kore wa nan desu ka*?" (What is this?) I asked while riding the train. "*Sore wa tokei desu.*" (That is a watch.) Terry answered. "*Kore wa nan desu ka*?" I asked again. "*Sore wa uma* (horse) *desu.*" You can imagine the looks on people's faces when they heard two foreigners asking themselves the same questions over and over again. Besides, there were no horses around. Are these men crazy? Are they already drunk at ten in the morning? I'm sure everybody was wondering. My conversations with Terry never went much further than that. "We have to find a Japanese native speaker to practice with us," I told the other members of the club at the next meeting.

やっと見つけた日本語ネイティブの練習相手

One day I met Noriko-*chan*, a very nice girl who wanted to help me. She spoke in Japanese all the time: "*Kore wa nan desu ka*?" or "*Anata wa ikutsu*?" (How old are you?) I understood her very well. She always spoke to me in a very simple way. I was happy. She was so sweet and nice to me. We met very often because she had a lot of free time. Sometimes we played together at the park. At other times we would go for an ice cream. I once asked her to have dinner with me, but her mother didn't let her go. "Is it because I'm a foreigner?" I asked her. She didn't seem to understand.

Suddenly, Noriko stopped coming to the park. Is she angry with me? Has her mother told her not to meet me anymore? I wondered sadly. I went to the park to look for Noriko many times, but she wasn't there. One day I learned from one of Noriko's mother's friends that the whole family had moved to another prefecture. I never saw her again. Even today I still remember nice Noriko. She was the best conversation partner I have ever had—and she was only four years old at the time.

It was already my second spring in Japan. The cherry blossoms (flowers) were everywhere. I wanted to forget my problems with the Japanese language for a while. My friends had told me that the best place for *hanami* (flower viewing) was Ueno Park. I decided to go. It was a wonderful sight—lots of pink flowers everywhere, and so many people happily drinking and singing. I began to search for a good place to sit, somewhere with a nice view and where there weren't too many drunks.

Then I saw a very beautiful girl in a kimono. She was standing alone by a cherry tree with her eyes closed. She looked as if she was thinking about the wonders of nature. I didn't care about the cherry blossoms anymore. I had to get closer to her. I wanted to talk and, if possible, arrange a date with her. The problem was, I didn't know what to say. My Japanese wasn't good enough. And I was afraid that she might not be able to speak any English at all. What could I do? After giving a little thought to the problem, I decided to do what Japanese had done to me.

"Excuse me, may I practice my Japanese with you?" I asked. She opened her eyes and looked into mine. Then she turned her eyes to the ground. Her face became red and she started to walk away. "Please stop!" I cried. "I only want to practice Japanese." She rolled up her kimono and began to run. I guess that by the time you read this, she will have arrived in Siberia.

ヒアリング練習は忍耐、忍耐

Much time has passed since my university days. My ability to speak Japanese has improved, but only a little. I can say the things I want to, but only in a simple, bookish way. Sometimes it's very much like "Tarzan" language: "Me want this. You open door," and so on. I feel sorry for the people who have to put up with my simple Japanese.

Thinking about this, I went to the barber shop close to my house. I told the lady there about my problem. "Do you have any suggestions?" I asked her. She looked at me and said, "You can stop worrying. I'll teach you Japanese *desu yo*! You can practice with me whenever you want to, *ne*." I thanked her, but I was not very happy about the idea. She wasn't very pretty and she was quite old. I'd rather practice while having a date with a pretty young lady, I thought. But remembering my experience at Ueno Park, I realized that it wasn't such a good idea after all.

Ever since that visit to the barber shop, I've had to put up with the old lady. Well, to tell you the truth, I can't practice much Japanese with her either. She is always talking. She's like a tape recorder. All I can say is "*Hai, hai*" (Yes, yes) or "*Soo desu ne.*" (You are right.) But it hasn't been all bad. Now I think of myself as an expert in the use of these sayings. Besides, my hearing ability has improved a lot. And now I know a lot about the lives of my neighbors.

Renting a Piece of Tokyo

異国日本での
夢の一人暮らしの第一歩!

大学の寮で一年間暮らしたボルガさんは、
アパートを借りて住むことにしました。
場所はどこがいいか、どんな物件がいいか、夢は膨らみます。
代々木上原の不動産屋に行ってみると
英語を話すきれいな女性スタッフもいて、いざ物件選びは始まります。
でも、その家賃の高さにびっくり。
本当にこんな高い家賃、みんな払っているの?

One year at the university dormitory was enough. It was a comfortable place, but I was tired of sharing the six-*tatami*-mat room with another guy. Waiting in line to take a shower wasn't very exciting either.

It was time for me to move to my own place. I didn't have a lot of money, but I knew what I wanted. I wanted my new home to be in Tokyo, close to a subway or train station and not too far from Shinjuku and other important shopping areas.

一人暮らしの物件探し、スタート

After carefully studying the map of Tokyo, I decided that the area around Yoyogi Uehara Station was the right place for me.

It had a subway, the Chiyoda Line, and a train, the Odakyu Line.

The neighborhood was nice and quiet. Prices in the stores and restaurants were reasonable. Shinjuku was only ten minutes away. Shimokitazawa was even closer. That was the right place!

But I had a communication problem. My Japanese was not good enough to carry on a conversation. It was "restaurant Japanese" —just enough to ask for pizza or spaghetti at a restaurant. So, I had to go to a real estate agent (someone who sells or rents land and buildings) who could speak English, someone with lots of foreign customers. This meant I couldn't go to a little real estate office. I had to choose a big name. Some friends offered to come with me, but I wanted to do everything by myself. "English spoken. Our prices are reasonable," said the advertisement in one of the English language newspapers. This is the agent I've been looking for, I thought. I called them right away and set up an appointment for the following day. "Good morning, my name is Yumiko Tanaka." A very nice-looking girl in her mid-twenties wearing a very short skirt greeted me. "I will be taking care of your housing needs," she said. Her English was perfect.

Yumiko showed me to a large meeting room. Somebody else brought some cookies and British tea with lemon. "Do you prefer a house or an apartment?" she wanted to know. "I was thinking about an apartment," was my reply. "I have the right place for you," she said with a broad smile, while bringing a bunch of papers to her desk. "You can choose among these."

高級住宅地のマンション賃貸価格はケタ違い！

The apartments were really wonderful. One of them caught my attention. Three rooms. A living room so big that I could play table tennis in the middle and still be able to have a dance party. The kitchen was a dream. Two toilets. "I love this one. How much is it?" I asked, quite excited.

"You have made a very good choice! This is our suggestion of the month. The price is quite reasonable," said Yumiko as she began to look at some notes. "Yes, this is the one! The price is one million, three hundred thousand yen per month. When signing the contract you have to pay another six million, five hundred thousand. That makes seven million, eight hundred thousand yen." When I got the total number, a piece of the cookie I was eating got stuck in my throat. I couldn't stop coughing for several minutes. I spilled some of my tea on the table. My face went red.

"You made a mistake," I said. "I want to RENT an apartment. I wasn't thinking about buying one."

Miss Yumiko Tanaka looked at me very seriously and said, "This, sir, is the price you have to pay to rent the place." For a moment I had a wild idea that her salary as a maid for ten years was also included in the price. But I kept quiet because she did not look like she was joking.

"I was thinking of a place somewhat cheaper," I said, coughing, with a piece of cookie still in my throat. She asked about my budget (the amount I could pay). When I told her I would prefer a six-*tatami* apartment, she quickly took away the remaining cookies and the tea. "We don't bother with such cheap places," she said. "You'll have to go somewhere else. Have a good day." A big fellow showed me to the door.

I went back to the dormitory, crying for help. My roommate offered his assistance. He said his brother's father-in-law had a cousin whose mother knew a person in the real estate business. After one week, I had met all those people. My back was in great pain because of the countless times I had to bow to show them I was a good guy. My knees hurt terribly after so many hours of sitting on my toes. I wondered if it was really necessary to go through all that exercise just to rent a little place. "You have to develop some personal relationships before people can introduce you to someone else," my friend explained.

At last I got an appointment. My friend came with me to do the translating. The real estate guy, Mr. Hashimoto, could speak no English at all. The office was in a dirty building that was falling apart. The place was so small that the three of us could not fit in, so we had to talk outside. No tea and cookies. "Mr. Hashimoto is very excited because you are his first foreign customer," my friend told me. "He is going to show us a very special apartment. Let's go!"

支払能力に見合ったのは安アパートだった

When we got to the place I couldn't see anything special about it. The building was even older than his office. The room was on the second floor. I wasn't sure the chairs could stand my weight. Mr. Hashimoto opened the door. Two cockroaches ran away. No need to go inside further than that. From the door I could see everything.

"Is this the SPECIAL place?" I wanted to know. "Yes, very special. You have a toilet, a shower, and a small kitchen," my friend translated. "Mr. Hashimoto can show us other apartments, but most of them have no toilet," he went on. This one was so small, but the price was right. I really couldn't pay any more. There wasn't much to think about. Although I wasn't exactly happy, I rented it.

The following week, I moved in. From the window of my new home, I could see the tall buildings of Shinjuku. To my left was a five-story apartment building. One day, through a window on the third floor, I saw the pretty, English-speaking sales lady from the first real estate agent I visited. She was showing the apartment to a tall businessman wearing a dark suit. Some roaches played close to my feet. When I compared his situation to mine, a tear fell from my eyes.

I had one hope, however. My neighbor might be a very pretty lady. But I wasn't lucky. It was a guy with a big dog that smelled bad. There were some advantages, though. Sitting on the toilet, I could hear what people all over the building were talking about. That is where I get some of the material for my stories.

「住めば都」だね

Several years have passed. I am still in the same place. I don't think about moving away anymore. The apartment feels like home. The roaches are gone. The landlady is very kind. She always brings me *yakitori* for dinner, and makes me feel like part of her family. From the window, I still look over to the apartment on the third floor of the five-story building. The sales lady from the other real estate office shows the place to new people every six months. I can't avoid thinking about Tokyo's very high prices.

By the way, the guy with the dog moved away and a girl moved in. But I wasn't lucky. She is so fat that she has problems going through the door. And, she brought quite a few roaches with her.

Renting a Piece of Tokyo 45

Train Shock

地獄の通勤ラッシュを
やり過ごすには？

日本の電車については驚くことばかりのボルガさん。
寸分狂わぬ運行スケジュール、
「ドアが閉まります、ご注意ください」などの親切すぎるアナウンス、
そして何より大混雑のすし詰め電車。
特にラッシュアワーの光景は、外国人の目には
奇異を通り越して、まさに地獄絵。
でも「押し屋」さんまでいるのだから、もう乗らないわけにはいきません！

My friends back home are always asking me about Japan. So I write a lot of letters. Here is one of them.

Dear Marcelo,

How are you? Sorry for being so late in answering your last letter. I was kind of busy at the company. This time, I'll be telling you about Japanese trains.

Do you remember that joke about the guy who went to pick up his father at the train station? The guy knew that the trains are usually late, so he went to the station one hour after the scheduled time for arrival. Just as he reached the platform, a train arrived. I am very lucky, I won't have to wait, he thought. In less than thirty minutes, all the people from the train were gone. But, the guy's father wasn't there. Rather worried, he walked over to an old man selling tickets and asked, "Excuse me sir, is this the nine o'clock train?"

"Yes, it is."

"I expected my father to come on this train, but he didn't. Please call the other station and find out if he had any problems."

"When was your father supposed to arrive?"

"Today, July 25, on the nine o'clock train."

"I can't see your problem," the old man said. "Your father will be coming tomorrow!"

"How do you know?"

"Very simple. This is yesterday's nine o'clock train."

恐るべし通勤地獄の実況中継

Well, Marcelo, trains here in Japan are very different. They are always on time. Sometimes they are late, but only a few minutes—unless a major earthquake has occurred. Difficult to believe, isn't it? But it's the truth.

Trains in Tokyo are as crowded as in any other major city of the world. That's not news. However, the *oshiya* (pushers) are something to talk about. Their job is to push, I would say pack, people into trains. They also signal the train driver with a little flag.

The other day I was standing in the middle of a platform in Shinjuku Station, waiting for a friend. Suddenly I started to move towards a train. I wasn't walking, but the crowd I was in kept moving. An *oshiya* was doing his job. I tried to escape, with no success. The doors closed and the train left with me inside. I was so angry that at the last moment I took the pusher's little red flag right out of his hand. When I got back to Shinjuku, my friend was quite angry because I was late. I told him what had happened, but he didn't believe me until I showed him the flag.

Once, I was riding a train during rush hour. Every time it went around a curve, my hands landed on the hips of a young lady standing in front of me. She didn't say a word the first and the second time, but finally she shouted in a very loud voice: "Do you want something with my skirt? You dirty pig!" Trains are crowded, but people ride in silence, so everybody heard her.

My face got red. I tried to move away, but I couldn't. "Don't even dream about touching my girlfriend again or I'll kill you!" a tall guy standing next to me said. The train stopped, the doors opened and I got off, although it wasn't my station. I was terribly ashamed. What should I do with my hands? I wondered. Perhaps on my chest? No! I might have the same problem, touching someone's chest! Since then I've concluded that the only safe place for my hands is on my head.

空いていても快適とは限らない日本の電車

Another time, although the train wasn't very crowded, a very *yakuza* (gangster) type of guy began to push me with his elbow. It was painful, so I tried to make room for him to pass by. But he just kept pushing. Finally, I managed to move to one side and stand behind him. At the next station, just as he was getting off, I caught his leg with my umbrella making him fall on the platform. Other people were also getting off the train, so he could not see me. The doors closed. A businessman standing next to him was carrying an umbrella. The poor man didn't know why the *yakuza* got so mad at him.

Stations are quite noisy. Just before a train closes its doors, a bell rings. Lately, at some stations, you can hear music instead of the bell. Actually, it's part of a *koto* concert, a very small part. I spent one morning standing on the platform, hoping to hear the whole concert. Unfortunately they always play the same little part.

There are lots of announcements inside the trains. "Sit straight! Don't stretch your legs! Give your seat to older people! Open windows! Close windows!" and many more.

Sometimes the announcements are translated. For example, in the "bullet train" the Japanese announcement is very long, but the English translation comes out quite short. A sweet voice says, "Have a nice trip." I wonder if they are trying to hide something we foreigners should know. Or could it be that they are saying bad things about us?

車内での人間ウォッチングはおもしろい

People traveling in trains usually read books or magazines. I love reading over their shoulders. There was a guy who used to ride the train with me every day at the same time. He always carried the same thick magazine and read a few pages each day. It was a very interesting story. I waited all day just to ride the train and continue reading. One day, he wasn't there. I've been looking for him, with no luck. It's been more than two months. So, if you are reading this, please be good and ride the train once more! There were only five pages left!

There are many other things I can tell you about. For example, the drunks trying to sleep on my back, the girls sitting with their faces covered with hair, the gangsters sitting on two seats, little children always pointing at me, university students carrying surf boards and knocking people's heads...but it's quite late already. I must go to bed. Write soon. Bye bye.

Your friend,
Fun Volga

Sweet Melodies of Love

セレナーデを歌う
ラテン式求愛の成果は？

日本に来て間もないころ、大学の料理クラブで知り合った
かわいい女の子に目を奪われたボルガさん。
何とかしてアプローチしたいと思い、ちょっと変わった方法、いえ、
ボルガさんのお国では求愛の常套手段である
セレナーデを歌うことにしました。
ある深夜、彼女の家の庭に忍び込み、
彼女が眠る部屋の窓の下で歌い始めたところ…

Shortly after coming to Japan, I joined a cooking club at my university, even though I hate cooking.

One of the club members, Mieko-*chan*, had caught my eye. I was very eager to talk with her, but I couldn't get her attention. Then, one day, I had an idea: what about doing something different, something really romantic? I decided to sing to her.

First, I had to find a guitar. But none of my friends had one. Just as I was about to give up, Yoshitaka, who lived in the dormitory room next to mine, brought me something with three strings.

"It's my mother's *shamisen*," he said. "You can have it for one night. But be extra careful. It's really expensive. My mother will be very angry if anything happens to it."

"No problem," I replied. I didn't know if I could play a nice love song with a *shamisen*, but it was the closest thing to a guitar I could find. Now, all I needed was Yoshitaka's bicycle. I told him I had to arrive at Mieko's house late at night, after the trains had stopped running. The idea of a serenade, I explained, is to wake up your beloved with a beautiful song.

深夜、自転車に乗って、いざ愛の告白に！

The following night, I rode the bicycle to Seijo Gakuen Mae, where Mieko lived, arriving long after midnight. It was too dark to see very well. But I knew where her house was, because I had gone looking for it a few days before.

I climbed the high stone wall surrounding her house. From the top of the wall I could see a row of old pines in the garden. There was a gentle breeze, and the pine branches seemed to be kissing each other, adding romance to the night. The house was completely dark. Perfect!

I jumped down into the garden and hurried to the house. Standing directly under Mieko's window, I began to sing. It was a song I had written especially for her:

You're so lovely that you make the stars grow pale.
When the moon sees your face, it hides behind a cloud.

A light came on in her room. She's heard me! I told myself, and went on singing. The window opened. "What's all that noise down there?" shouted a fat woman with white cream all over her face.

"Please call Mieko. I'm singing for her," I shouted back. How could she call my beautiful singing "noise"? I began to sing louder: *You're so pretty that...*

The woman left the window and came back carrying a big bucket of water. "Go away. I want to sleep!" she screamed, and poured the water over me.

Now I was mad. "I want to see Mieko!" I shouted.

I was so busy shouting and singing that I didn't notice the man with the baseball bat. He was running toward me. "Hey you," he shouted, "stop bothering my wife!"

"I'm not moving until I see Mieko-*chan*," I said, as bravely as I could.

The guy swung the bat at me. I had to protect my head...with the *shamisen*. CRASH! It broke in two. "Stop! Stop!" I shouted. "There's no need to be violent." But the guy kept coming. I took several quick steps backwards, hit a rock, and fell into some plants with sharp points. "OUCH!"

"You spoiled my wife's cactus garden," said the man, with a terrible look in his eyes. Now he was really mad.

I climbed over the wall and ran away as fast as I could, with cactus needles sticking in my rear. Riding home on the bicycle was quite painful. My pride was hurt, and so was my bottom.

恋愛も「郷に入っては郷に従え」だって

When I got back to the dormitory, I went straight to Yoshitaka's room and turned on the light.

"Who...what's ...Fun? It's 3:30 in the morning. What happened?"

I showed him my sore bottom.

"Wow," he said sympathetically.

"Here, lie down on your stomach. I'll get some medicine." I lay down on the rug.

"I guess now you know why we don't serenade girls in Japan," he said, laughing. "By the way, where's my mother's *shamisen*?"

"Well, I had to protect myself," I said, holding up the little piece I still had. He slapped me hard on the bottom and went back to bed.

The next day, I asked Mieko why she hadn't come to the window when I sang to her.

She looked surprised. "Our next-door neighbors told us about a crazy foreigner who wrecked their cactus garden last night," she said. "Was that you?"

That was the last time I tried to introduce Latin romance and passion to Japan.

Osaka in White

日本では結婚披露宴まで
儀式みたい？

初めて日本の結婚披露宴に招待されたボルガさん。
3カ月も前に招待状と新幹線チケットが送られてきました。
アルゼンチンで行われた
カジュアルでフレンドリーな妹の結婚パーティーを思い出しつつ、
いざ勇み足で遠路、大阪へ。
当日、用意してきたオコメを新郎新婦に
「おめでとう！」とふりかけてみたら…

"Would you like to come to my wedding?" Sachiko asked me over the phone some time ago. She was calling from Osaka. "Yes," I answered. "I'll be very happy to come. I'm going to get my Shinkansen tickets tomorrow morning!" I was excited. That was the first time I had ever been invited to a real Japanese wedding. "You don't have to hurry," said Sachiko. "The wedding will be in three months." "Three months! That's a long time to wait," I told her. "I don't know if I'll be in Japan three months from now." "Don't worry," Sachiko continued. "You can think it over. I'll send you a card in two days, and you answer me by mail."

Exactly two days later I received the invitation, a Shinkansen ticket, and a map showing the way from Osaka Station to the Midori Kaikan, the hall where the wedding party would take place. Reading the invitation, I learned that the party would begin at three o'clock. I had a week to say whether I would go or not, by drawing a circle around some kanji on a card and sending it back to Osaka. That was very well-planned. I wondered how different a wedding in Japan would be from the ones I knew.

祖国アルゼンチンの結婚式

I still remember very clearly when one of my sisters got married. She sent the invitation letters only three weeks in advance. I thought even that was too early, but women worry so much. Wedding presents started to arrive after one week. She received a refrigerator, towels, dishes, and many other useful presents.

On the wedding day, in the morning, she and her future husband went to the city office. After filling out the papers required by law, they were married.

However, the "real" wedding ceremony took place in a big Catholic church during a mass. It lasted a little over an hour. There were lots of guests. When the mass was finished, the couple came out of the church, and everybody began to throw rice at them. I had never seen that in Japan. Is it because rice is too expensive?

My sister and her husband rode in a car. We all followed her in our own cars. There were about 300 guests, so you can imagine the number of cars. After going around the city for almost half an hour making a lot of noise, we arrived at the hall where the wedding party would be held. It was about 10:30 p.m. Everybody was happy. My sister looked really pretty in her white dress. My father and mother, as well as my sister's husband's parents, were sitting by her at the main table. The rest of the guests sat wherever they wished. The party began. We all ate a lot and took hundreds of pictures.

We usually dance the waltz after the dinner is over, just before the dessert. At about 1:30 a.m. the dance began. After an hour we returned to our seats to eat the wedding cake. By 3:00 p.m. the happy couple left. The party went on for two or three more hours.

Since Sachiko's wedding was to be my first in Japan, I did not expect it to be much different from my sister's wedding. To get ready for the big day, I went to the supermarket near my house and bought two kilograms of rice. I might eat some of it before the wedding day, but I thought that if I could take half a kilo with me to Osaka, it would be enough.

やっと来た晴れの日、日本式の結婚式に初めて列席！

Time passed very slowly. One month. Two months. At last the wedding day arrived. I woke up very early in the morning. I prepared the suit that I was going to wear for the wedding and left for Osaka. The trip on the Shinkansen was very enjoyable. It was a bright, sunny day. On the way, I could see Mount Fuji.

I arrived at Shin-Osaka Station at 11:00 a.m. I had plenty of time to get to the Midori Kaikan by three. However, I did not want to be late to my first Japanese wedding. Therefore, after leaving my suitcase in a coin locker, I took the train to Osaka Station.

The map Sachiko had sent me almost three months before a was very good one. I had no problem finding the Midori Kaikan. The people at the front desk were very surprised to see a foreigner coming in. However, they were very friendly. They told me the way to Sachiko's party in great detail. It was on the second floor. I had walked very slowly so it was already 1 o'clock in the afternoon. Since there were still two hours left, I bought a newspaper and sat in the lobby.

"The guests waiting for Miss Sachiko Tanaka and Mr. Taro Takahashi may go in now. The room is ready for the party to begin," a sweet voice announced over the loudspeakers.

よりによって遅刻とは?!

I checked my watch. It was only 1:25.

Japanese always worry about the time, I thought. I don't want to sit in the room for almost two hours with nothing to do. I think I'll wait a little more here before going in. Fifteen minutes later, I do not know why, I looked again at the invitation. My heart started to beat faster. I had made a big mistake. The time for the beginning of the party was 1:30. The people from the Midori Kaikan were not crazy. I ran as fast as I could. There was nobody left outside. The doors were closed. What could I do? I knocked. Nothing happened. I knocked again. An old man in a black suit came out, and after I explained my mistake, he let me in. Everybody was sitting, listening to a speech. I did not want anyone to see me, so

I sat in an empty seat close to the door. My first Japanese wedding, and I was late!

After five minutes, the man who had opened the door for me came back. I was in his place. "Your place is over there," he said, pointing to a chair very close to a huge wedding cake. The people looked at me as I walked to my seat. My face was completely red. I was carrying my camera and the rice I had brought from Tokyo. I am sure it was very funny, because some people laughed. I was very ashamed. Sachiko looked at me and smiled. She was wearing a colorful kimono. There was another very long speech. Then a third one. I was a little hungry.

母国の結婚披露宴との違いにびっくり！

At last we began to eat. The food was very Japanese. I remember eating something called *kombu* or something like that. It was terrible. Some people went on giving speeches during the meal, but I did not pay much attention to them. We had no speeches at my sister's party.

Everybody was still eating when Sachiko left the room. Maybe she wants to go to the toilet, I thought. Then, her husband also left. Two to the toilet? What a surprise! They came back in Western wedding clothes. My sister did not change clothes at her wedding!

We had already finished with the meal. I was waiting for the cake. You know—after the *kombu*. Sachiko and her husband took a big knife and walked over to the cake and looked as if they were cutting it. But they did not cut it! In fact they went back to their seats. Hey! They forgot the waltz. Then I looked around the room. There was no place for the dance. We would have to throw the tables out of the window. More photos and the party was over. And the cake?

I was so close to the cake, and with such a bad taste in my mouth because of the *kombu*, that I could not help it, I put my hand out toward the cake. I wanted to taste the frosting (topping). I guess you can imagine my surprise. The cake was made of plastic!!

When I went out of the room, Sachiko was standing by the door. Then I remembered the rice. In a second it was all over her. Sachiko screamed. The guests stopped talking. They all looked at me. No words. Those were the longest five seconds of my life. A man came over to me. "I am from the Midori Kaikan," he said. "In Japan, we do not throw the rice. We eat it!"

"I am sorry. I didn't know."

"Do not worry. Clean the floor!"

Then he left. I could hear him saying something like, "These foreigners are all crazy."

Meetings and More Meetings

退屈な会議を
楽しく過ごす方法とは？

来日してから日本の会社で働いて数年たったボルガさん。
あらゆる面で日本流が板についてきましたが、
ひとつだけどうしても慣れないものがあります。
それは頻繁に行われる「会議」。
長い時間をかけても何も決まらなかったり、
とても生産性があるとは思えない会議の時間を
有効に過ごすためにボルガさんが考え出したアイディアとは?!

I've been working for some years at a Japanese company. In the beginning, I had a few problems getting used to the different ways of "doing things." As time passed, I became used to them, but no matter how long I stay in this country there is something I will never get used to —meetings!

So far, I have discovered that one of the secrets of doing business in Japan is to have a lot of meetings. Every day if possible. This rule holds true no matter whether you are a foreigner or a Japanese. Everybody has to suffer. At the same time, it seems that Japanese-style meetings are special. Lots of people have to go. In fact, the more the better! Two or three persons might get together. But those are not real meetings. They are just little chats.

I remember a time when my boss said to me in his strongest voice, "Next month on the 17th we'll have our department meeting." The day before, he had sent each of us a piece of paper telling us the same thing. There are so few of us in our department that I always wonder why it is necessary to call a meeting at all. Yumiko, sitting in front of me, always gives me the same answer. "Meetings at Japanese companies are very formal events. We have to be serious about them." It seems she is right. Most of our meetings are planned at least one month before. I was told the reason is that everybody must be present.

日本の会社はミーティング至上主義？

There are almost no excuses for not going or being late to a meeting. Not long ago we were to have a meeting. I was sure that it would be boring (not interesting) as usual. I decided to be as late as possible. "Where have you been?" the boss asked. After the meeting, he scolded me for almost one hour about the importance of being on time for meetings.

Many times the subjects discussed at company meetings are very "serious." The following are some examples: how to use the new coffee machine; the job the guy sitting next to your desk is doing; the plans for the next company trip; and holiday schedules.

Mind you, everybody usually knows beforehand what might be said during a meeting. Either the guy sitting next to you talks about his job, or you have been using the new coffee machine for more than a month and you already know how to operate it. But no matter what the subject might be, there is a very good chance that you have already heard or read about it before.

ミーティングの時間を有効に過ごすための提案

The very few times something new is really said, the speaker is boring. You don't want to hear about it! So, during meetings, most people do one of the following things:

a) Sleeping: As I have said before, some people are so good at this that they can even sleep with their eyes open. I am trying to learn this skill, but it takes a long time to master. You can see at some meetings that the oldest man in the room is the first to fall sleep. The golden rule here is that you don't notice the snores (ZZZ...).

b) Playing with pencils by making them spin over your thumb: There is always someone who is learning, though. That is why you shouldn't show surprise if you see a few UFLOs (Unidentified Flying Long Objects) flying over the table.

c) Planning the next holiday: Most times the girls are reading guide books on Hawaii or Guam while trying to hide them behind Mickey Mouse or Donald Duck notebooks. Later, I ask them for tips for my next trip. But being OLs (office ladies), they've only seriously studied the fashion boutiques (clothes shops) and restaurants—I can use the restaurant dining information—but I could never find anything to fit me in those boutiques.

d) Smoking: If you don't smoke, you had better learn how to. During meetings, the air is so full of smoke that you can't see the faces around you. The smoke is great for hiding the faces of those sleeping, so they are never discovered. By the way, I must add here that, thanks to meetings, I have mastered the art of making little rings with smoke. My next challenge is trying to make an *a*. I have decided not to stop until I can blow out all the letters of the alphabet from *a* to *z*.

e) Research: Trying to find out if the girl sitting in front of you has a boyfriend or not. Sometimes it's difficult, but I enjoy the challenge. The other possibility is finding a good drinking spot for the evening. Those two are my favorite subjects!

f) Listening: This is only for the new workers during their first three months in the company. Later they will learn how to smoke or play with their pencils. They are still too young to sleep or have too little money to think about trips.

国によって違う？ ミーティングすることの意味

During meetings very few decisions are made—except for the date and time of the next meeting. If there is a real need to make a decision, a separate meeting with more people will be arranged. Before the meeting, your job is to talk to each member who will attend that meeting. You will get their opinions and ideas so you can prepare an offer everybody will agree with. If you've done your work well, there will be no need to talk during that meeting. When you come to think about this system, it has one important good point—you can catch up with your sleep!

When the meeting is over, the first ones to leave are those who were smoking. They have to buy more cigarettes. The guys playing with their pens have to stay a little longer looking under the table or chairs for their UFLOs. The girls have the job of picking up the green-tea cups from the table. This is very important, because they have to make as much noise as possible so as to wake up those still sleeping.

Mind you, I do not want to make you think that ALL meetings are like this one. Sometimes, but not very often, they are interesting. You learn something new, decisions are made, or there are even some real discussions. I guess the main problem for me is that I am too used to Western-style meetings. Those are real fun. There is more talking—and even some fighting!

I have to stop here. The guy sitting next to my desk has just told me that I must leave right now. I have to go to today's third "important" meeting. Next time I promise to tell you about meetings with foreign visitors. They are the most entertaining! By the way, I would love to hear about your experiences in meetings. Do you have a different feeling about meetings or have you had any funny things happen?

Who Cares?

ビジネスでのカルチャー・ギャップはもっときつい?!

初来日したイタリア人フランコに
日本のビジネス・スタイルを伝授したボルガさん。
個人的な関係が重要視されること、物事を決めるのに時間がかかること、
責任の所在がはっきりしないこと、などなど。
でも「そんなの時間の無駄だ!」と一蹴したフランコは
我流で日本のビジネス・シーンに臨みましたが、
うまくいったのでしょうか?

I was at the office getting ready to eat my box lunch, when the phone rang. "Hello, Mr. Volga?" said a hurried voice. And before I could answer, "My name is Franco Taglioretti. I just arrived from Italy, and tomorrow morning I have a meeting at one of the main Japanese clothing companies. I've heard that you give advice, so I'd like some. We have to meet!"

"I'm sorry, but I'm busy this evening," I said.

"I see. Well then, tell me something right now, something helpful for my meeting."

I tried to think. "Personal relationships are very important," I said. "Doing business can take a long time."

"I don't agree," said Franco, his voice becoming louder. "In business you have to push!"

"Perhaps it isn't a good idea to push too much," I suggested. "Japanese usually take a long time to make a decision so that..."

"That doesn't make any sense," he said, not letting me finish. "Why does it take so long?"

"Because they want as many people as possible to say something about the decision before it is made. That way, if something goes wrong, they can say it was everybody's decision and everybody can feel bad together. Japanese like to do things together."

"Sounds like a waste of time to me."

日本人との商談なら、お任せあれ！？

It was difficult to advise someone who thought he knew everything. But I felt I should do my best to help him. "Be careful with interpreters. Sometimes they aren't very good."

"Isn't it their job to be good?"

"Well, yes. But let me give you an example. A few weeks after I started my job, the *kacho* called me. Our president was going to meet with an American businessman who wanted our company to help sell his company's products in Japan. The *kacho* asked me to be the interpreter at the meeting. Of course, I couldn't say no."

"Yes, yes. I don't want to hear a story. Tell me how the meeting went."

"It went very well until we got to the part where our president asked the American businessman what he wanted to sell in Japan. The businessman said, 'I would like you to help me import fruit.' But I said *keda-*

mono (wild animals) instead of *kudamono* (fruit). The president's mouth fell open—very un-Japanese. And the rest of the conversation, with my help, went like this:

President: ' It will be a little difficult, I think.'

Businessman: 'What's so difficult about it? Don't Japanese like to eat delicious wild animals? In my country we like to put them on our corn flakes in the morning. Wild animal salads are good, too. Don't you think so?'

President: 'Thank you very much for taking the time to come here and visit us. We will think carefully about everything you have said.'

"And that was the end of the meeting."

"Japanese are very strange," said Franco. "If I were the president, I would have fired you right there."

日本流のビジネスに慣れておかないとね

I'm sure you would have, I thought. But I continued to give him advice. "Shake hands gently and don't slap people on the back. Don't write notes on people's business cards while they're talking to you. Wait until they leave the room. A girl will serve you tea that is green and too hot. If you can't drink it, pour it into the nearest potted plant when no one is looking. And don't try to date the girl who brings the tea." But he didn't pay any attention and finally, after telling me when we would meet again, he hung up the phone.

Two days later we met in Shibuya. "How was your meeting?" I asked him.

Franco began to wave his arms as though they were flags. "There were so MANY of them!" he shouted. "First, there was the president. Then another guy called Waganabe came in, followed by Yamamono."

"You mean Watanabe and Yamamoto."

"That's what I said. Anyway, whatever their names were, there were a lot of them. And they just kept coming in and shaking my hand. I got really tired."

"That's why people bow here in Japan. It isn't as tiring as shaking hands. However, bowing is very difficult to learn. Japanese start practicing from the time they are babies." I was very proud of my deep understanding of Japanese culture, but Franco wasn't interested.

"Why did they call in so many people?" he demanded to know.

"They wanted you to feel welcome and also, it was a good opportunity for a free English lesson. Did you...?" He didn't let me finish.

"Well, they didn't practice speaking English very much. They just sat there and sucked air, making a strange noise."

日本でのビジネスは疲れるだけでなく危険をもはらむ？！

"They were trying to show you that they were thinking carefully about what you were saying. Or, they were thinking about the noodles they were going to eat for lunch. Or..."

"Sure, sure, whatever. Anyway, after the air sucking noises, the president spoke for about two minutes in Japanese, and the interpreter said, 'Welcome to Japan.' I said, 'Wait! Are you translating EVERYTHING?' The guy started smiling and bowing and drinking his tea. He looked really upset. But I wasn't worried about that, I wanted to start talking business."

"But..."

"But all they wanted to know was what foods I could eat. Did I like raw fish? Could I use chopsticks? Finally they ran out of questions. After a long silence and some more air sucking, the president introduced his company and I introduced mine. Well, I thought, now we'll get started. But a girl came in and announced that it was lunchtime. The meeting was over. I couldn't believe it!"

I was about to tell Franco not to hurry so much, when I saw the big bandage around his hand. "What happened to you?" I asked.

"After the meeting they were going to take me to a restaurant," he answered. "A taxi was waiting in front of the building. I didn't want to waste any more time, so I hurried to open the door. But the door suddenly opened by itself, hitting my hand. Doing business in this country not only takes too long, it can be dangerous!"

"I hope you're OK," I said. But later, riding home on the train, I thought: That's what happens to people who don't listen to me.

International Business

海外出張でハプニングに見舞われる！

日本で働き始めて9年目にして、
初めての海外出張に行くことになったボルガさん。
行き先はオーストラリアで、有頂天になったものの、
事前準備のため、連日の深夜残業にクタクタ。
それでもいざ勇んで飛行機に乗り込んだボルガさんは、
さっそくカルチャー・ギャップや、
オーストラリア英語に戸惑う羽目に…

"Fun, I've always wanted to travel overseas on business, but my boss doesn't give me the chance," said my friend Masayo-*chan,* sadly. She turned back to her PC. "It isn't really that exciting," I said, looking over her shoulder at the numbers jumping around on the screen.

"You're only saying that to make me feel better."

"No, it's the truth! Listen, I just came back from a business trip to Australia and believe me, it's nothing like the stories you might have heard."

Masayo-*chan* didn't believe me. So I decided to tell her about my business trip. A few weeks ago my manager called me to his desk. "Fun-*chan*," he said, "I'm sending you to Australia to visit a company that is interested in buying our products and..."

初めての海外出張に浮かれすぎて…

"I'm ready to go!" I interrupted. For the first time in nine years, I was going on a business trip, and the company was going to pay for it. I was so happy! I ran around the office telling everyone about the great time I was going to have and the wonderful presents I would buy.

When I got back to my desk, however, my manager was waiting for me. "Volga-*kun*," he said, "this is a business, not a travel agency. You'll be our face in Australia and you had better be well-prepared." He handed me a 10-cm-high pile of papers. "Read these carefully and write a report for our Australian customers." The rest of the week I had to work late every night. Twice I slept on some chairs in the office.

By the time I got on the plane, I was so nervous that I had to read a "salaryman" *manga* to relax. Sitting in the seats next to me were a little Australian boy and his mother. The little boy kept looking at me. Finally he turned to his mother and said, "Look, Mom, he's not a kid, but he's reading a comic book."

"Archie," his mother whispered angrily. "Keep quiet! He's going to hear you. And don't point at people; it's bad manners."

I pretended not to notice.

"Hey mister," said the little boy, "can I read your comic book?"

"Well," I said, "it's not really a comic for little kids."

"What do you mean it's not for kids? Gimme!" he cried, pulling the *manga* book away from me and leaving a couple of torn pages in my hand.

"Look, Mom, look!" he shouted. "There's a man and a woman with no clothes on!"

"What IS this?" his mother asked coldly, taking the *manga* away from her son.

"Comics are a form of art in Japan," I explained proudly. "We salarymen read them to learn how to behave in various situations. For example, this one here is a tender story about a salaryman and an 'OL' who got tired of working overtime."

"Archie, don't talk to that man," she ordered.

I turned my head toward the window and pretended to sleep. If Australians are this hard to get along with, I wondered, how will I be able to make a good impression on the business people I'm meeting in Sydney tomorrow?

不慣れなオージー・イングリッシュに混乱！

The next day, a Friday, I had an afternoon meeting with the president of the Australian company and his staff. They were in a hurry to talk business. But I had learned in Japan that it's necessary to go drinking together before anything serious can be discussed. So I told them what a great country Australia is and suggested that, after the meeting, we go to a karaoke bar.

Looking a little bit surprised, the president said, "I'll be having dinner with my Sheila today. You can go with my staff."

"Your Sheila? You mean your dog?" I asked.

"No, my wife," he answered, a little upset. Fortunately, Bob, the vice president, explained that I wasn't familiar with Australian English.

The president understood, and to show he wasn't angry, he said, "Tomorrow I'm having a barbecue party at my house. I'll pick you up at the hotel at eight in the morning."

It was easy to find a karaoke bar in Sydney and soon we were having a great time. Bob had just finished singing "Down Under" and was in a good mood. "OK, mates," he cried out. "It's my shout!"

Not again, I told myself. His singing is terrible! I leaned closer to him and very politely said, "Bob, I think you've shouted enough. Now, you should let someone else sing." He didn't talk to me for the rest of the evening and left before everyone else. Later I found out that in Australia, "It's my shout" means, "It's my turn to buy the drinks."

But I soon forgot about it. The rest of us kept drinking and singing at the karaoke bar until the owner told us to leave because it was closing time. Then we went to a park and stayed there, drinking all night.

When the sun came up, I suddenly realized that the president was going to pick me up at the hotel in two hours. "I should be going, mates," I said. "Thanks for everything."

憧れの海外出張のエンディングは…

I walked in circles back to the hotel. Tired and quite drunk, I opened the door of my room and turned on the lights. I took off my clothes, threw them on the floor, and went into the bathroom to take a shower. I closed the door behind me and reached for the mirror. "Hey! Where's my toothbrush and the soap?" I said. "Where's the mirror?" All I could see was a picture hanging on the wall.

Something is wrong here! I thought. This isn't my bathroom! Looking around, I realized I was standing in the middle of the hallway with no clothes on. I tried to go back into my room but the door was locked. Of course, I had no key. I had to cover myself with something and go get another one. I thought about using the picture but it was nailed to the wall. The carpet was too big.

With my face toward the wall, I walked sideways to the supply room. Luckily I found some sheets. I wrapped my body like a Roman emperor and rushed down to the lobby. The guy at the front desk tried very hard not to laugh when he asked, "May I help you, Mr. Volga?" My face was very red.

At that moment, the president walked in with his wife and son. "Look, look, Daddy," shouted the little boy. "That's the man who showed me the pictures on the plane!" The president turned around and quickly led his family out of the hotel.

I didn't have to tell Masayo-*chan* that my business trip was unsuccessful. "Poor Fun," she said. "It'll probably be another nine years before your manager lets you go overseas again."

"It'll probably be another nine years before he speaks to me again," I replied.

"Well anyway, thank you for the advice," she said. "I feel much better now. I realize that traveling for pleasure is much more fun."

A Dog in
My Life

犬は飼い主に忠誠を
尽くすのではなかったの？

友人から、一目ぼれした近所の女性に
どうやってアプローチしたらいいのか相談されたボルガさん。
実は最近、自分の恋愛はまったくの不振続きで、
デートにすらこぎつけられません。
でも、友人の頼みとあっては何とかしなくては！と思いついたのが、
まずはその女性の飼い犬を手なずける、という作戦。
うまくいくのでしょうか？

Last April I was walking around Ginza when someone began shouting my name. To tell the truth, I was rather tired and didn't feel like talking to anyone, so I ran to a subway entrance. But as I started down the stairs, a hand caught my arm.

"What's wrong, Fun, didn't you hear me?" the guy asked.

It was Seto Hayashi. I had met him when I was working part-time as a Spanish translator. "Seto, what a surprise!" I said.

"Fun, I've heard you're a part-time consultant now. You have to help me!"

I didn't have time to answer. He pulled me to a nearby bench. "I'm in love!" he said, placing his hands over his heart.

"Good for you," I said. "Who is she?"

"I don't know," he answered, looking down at his shoes.

"What do you mean, you don't know?"

"Well, I know her, but I don't. I've seen her many times in my neighborhood, but I can't talk to her. That's why I need your help. Please!"

もてないボクに恋愛の相談をするなんて…

Seto was holding my arm with both hands and shaking it. I couldn't think clearly. Of course I wanted to help, but all my recent approaches to girls had been terrible failures. I was about to tell him to ask someone else when suddenly, I remembered something.

"Does she have a dog?"

"Yes, a big, ugly-looking one, but..."

"Your problem is solved. Listen carefully. You have to become good friends with the dog. Buy a thick, juicy steak every day. Go to her house at night while everybody is asleep, and give it to the dog."

"I don't want to date the dog!"

"Let me finish. Keep feeding steaks to the dog for about two weeks, until it remembers you. Then follow the girl and find out where she takes the dog for a walk every day. When you walk past her, the dog will recognize you and come over to you. When she sees that the dog likes you, she'll start a conversation."

Before I could say, "You're welcome," he was on his way to the nearest supermarket to buy the first steak.

Two weeks later, at 6 o'clock on a Sunday morning, I heard someone banging on my front door. With one eye closed and the other eye half-open, I walked to the door. Opening it, I saw a very dirty guy. He was breathing loudly. His hair was a mess, and his clothes were torn. A drunk! I thought, and closed the door quickly.

Ring, ring, ring, bang, bang, bang! He wouldn't go away. I got really angry. I picked up an umbrella, opened the door again, and shouted, "Listen, if you don't go away, ..."

"Fun, it's me, Seto," said the dirty guy.

"Seto! Please, come in and sit down. What happened to you?"

"I followed YOUR advice!" he said angrily. "I fed expensive steaks to the dog for two weeks, just as you suggested. Then I walked past the girl in a park. When the dog saw me, it jumped on me. She apologized, and we started a nice conversation. But as soon as the dog realized I didn't have any steaks, it got angry and bit me. My bottom is still sore."

"Maybe the dog thought your bottom was a high-quality steak," I said, trying to make a joke.

"This isn't funny!" Seto shouted. "She couldn't control the dog. It started jumping up at me, trying to bite me all over. I had to run away, and the dog ran after me. In fact, I've been running all night and..."

犬をキューピットに仕立て上げようとしたけれど…

"Wan, wan, grrrrr, wan, wan." A very unfriendly dog was outside scratching at my front door.

"Oh no, it found me!" Seto cried in a frightened voice. "Do something, Fun!"

"I'm not a dog consultant," I said politely. "I only give advice about love problems."

That was not what Seto wanted to hear. With a dangerous look in his eyes, he took hold of my collar. "You got me into this mess," he said. "I'm not moving until you get me out of it."

"OK, relax," I said. "I'll think of something." But I didn't know what to do. The last time I tried to be friendly to a dog, its owner hit me with a plastic bag full of smelly dog stuff.

I was remembering that terrific smell and listening to the dog scratching at my front door, when the phone rang. It was the owner of the apartment building. "Do you know what time it is?" he asked me in an angry voice. "It's six in the morning. I can't sleep. You know pets aren't permitted in this building. Either the dog leaves, or you do." He hung up the phone without giving me a chance to explain the situation. I had to do something.

"Seto, get ready to go out the window," I said. Opening my refrigerator, I took out a slice of ham, two sausages, and a salami. It was all I had, but it didn't seem like enough. So I added a banana for dessert.

When I opened my front door, the dog showed two rows of sharp, yellow teeth. But as soon as it saw the salami, it calmed down. While the dog was eating, Seto jumped out of the window and ran home. After the dog finished eating, it went away too, without even looking at me.

結局、ボクの恋愛アドバイスは成功したのだが…

That night Seto called. "Fun, you're a genius! I've got a date."

"Congratulations. What happened?"

"When I got home, Itsumi, that's her name, was waiting for me. She wanted to apologize. By the way, have you seen her dog? It hasn't come home yet."

I was about to say no, when I heard a scratching sound at my front door. "Wan, wan, grrrr, wan, wan."

"It didn't come home because it's still here," I said, "right outside my door. You have to help me. Please!"

"Sorry, Fun," he replied. "I hate dogs. Bye."

Five months have passed since that day. Seto and Itsumi are still dating, and they plan to get married next month. Meanwhile, my life has changed a lot. The dog comes to my door every night. I've spent all my money buying it food. Do you know a girl who would like to approach me? If you do, please tell her to make friends with the dog.

Lines into the Future

占いにばかり
頼ってはいられません!

もともと占いには興味のなかったボルガさん。
でも会社帰りに、同僚の女性たちにけしかけられ、
道端の占い師に手相を見てもらったところ、
どうやら金運がいいらしい。
すっかり気をよくしたボルガさんは占いに凝りだし、
今度は原宿の占いの館にまで出かけましたが、
占いの結果を早合点して、またも空回りする羽目に…

One evening, I was talking with three of my co-workers in our office in Akasaka-Mitsuke. "Fun, what do you mean, no one has ever read your hands?" Makiko looked very surprised. "Don't you want to know if you're going to die a *sarariman*?" Toshiko asked. "And what about marriage?" added Mieko, turning a little pink.

"Girls, girls, I don't believe in fortune-telling."

"Let me see!" Makiko said, grabbing my hands. The other two crowded in around her for a closer look. "The marriage line isn't clear," whispered Mieko in a disappointed voice.

"We'd better talk to a professional," said Makiko. Before I could respond, they were pulling me out of the building. "Let's go to 'Shinjuku's Mama'," said Toshiko, pushing me to the right. "No, no, 'Ginza's Papa' is better," insisted Mieko, pulling my arm the other way. Makiko added her ideas. Soon, a long list of mamas, papas, grandmas, and grandpas had been suggested.

同僚の女性に付き合わされた占いに意外にもはまって…

"What about him?" I said, pointing to a middle–aged man sitting by a little table in front of a bank. The others agreed, and I asked the man how much he charged.

"Basic information, ¥3,000," he replied, staring up at the stars.

"Three? No way!" I tried to leave, but the girls pushed me back. I had to pay.

"As a child, you were very bad," he began, looking at my hands with one eye and his watch with the other. "You're good at pretending to be intelligent," he continued, "and..."

"Never mind all that," interrupted Toshiko. "What about money?"

"This line here shows a lot of success," he said.

"Are you sure?" I asked, beginning to get interested.

"Yes. Many company presidents, famous writers, and other successful people have this line."

I'm a famous writer, I thought.

"What about marriage?" Mieko asked.

"Later," I said. "When will the money start to flow in?"

"Sometime in the future. But first, you're going to spend more money than you'd planned."

I was wonderfully happy. I was going to be rich! From that day on, I didn't care about saving money. I was too busy spending it, just as the fortune-teller had said. But I wasn't getting any richer. My bank account just got smaller and smaller. I started to worry, and the next time I saw Mieko I told her I was thinking about going to another fortune-teller and getting a second opinion. She, too, was eager to have her fortune told, so she came with me.

This time we went to a house near Harajuku. We entered a darkened room and saw a lady dressed in Middle Eastern clothes. She was sitting in front of a crystal ball, her face half covered by a handkerchief. "Sit down and look into the ball with me," she ordered. She began to sing a strange melody and yellow smoke flowed from a corner of the room. I held my nose and tried to keep from laughing.

Suddenly, she turned to Mieko. "Yes, I see it!" she shouted. "Marriage is waiting for you!" Mieko smiled a warm smile. "What about me?" I asked. "When am I going to get rich?" "You will marry a nice tall man," she continued saying to Mieko, pretending not to hear me.

"But what about my money?" "No money!" she replied in an angry voice and turned again to Mieko. "The man of your dreams is close to you. He's a foreign writer living in Japan." She was talking about me!

もっとわかりやすく占ってください!

Later, as we left the fortune-teller's house, Mieko was humming a happy little tune. But I was worried. No money and marriage to Mieko? I didn't even like her. The fortune-teller must have made a mistake. Then, suddenly, I remembered. "Mieko, isn't your father the owner of a big construction company?" I asked.

"Yes, he's got tons of money."

So this was how I was supposed to get rich. "Well, then, I guess the fortune-teller was right," I said, trying to sound romantic. "We should see each other more often, don't you think?"

"I'd love to, Fun. You're funny. But my boyfriend, Bob, just finished his book, and he wants me to take a vacation with him. Now that I know he's going to marry me, I think I'll go. See you later." 🌹

Night Hunter

リサイクルよりエコロジカル？
粗大ゴミの再利用！

あるとき洗濯機が壊れてしまい、なるべく早く安く買おうとしたところ、
ショッピング・アドバイザーの友人ローランドに、
ディスカウント・ショップよりも安い「店」に案内されました。
そこは粗大ゴミ収集所。
ためらいはあったけれど、とにかく洗濯物を手洗いする生活から脱したい！
そこで、早朝に二人して出かけてみると、
ありました、洗濯機が…

Not long ago, I went to several discount stores looking for a new washing machine. The prices were lower than they used to be, but still too high for me. I explained the problem to Roland, my shopping adviser.

"I know the cheapest store in town," he said. "You name it, the 'garbage store' has it."

By "garbage store" he meant the *sodai-gomi* that people put out on non-burnable garbage day.

Digging around in people's garbage would be embarrassing, but I was in a hurry to get a washing machine. I had been washing by hand for so long that my skin was falling off. I suggested that we go early in the morning so that no one would see us.

目当ての品を求め、いざ粗大ゴミ収集所に！

On the next non-burnable garbage day, well before sunrise, I met Roland at my subway station. We started walking through my neighborhood. I had high hopes, but after an hour of searching the only thing I found was a useless wooden tray. Then, just as I was about to give up, I saw it—a washing machine!

It was near a garbage collection place, outside an apartment building. Even in the darkness, I could tell that the washing machine was garbage because it was dirty. The people in the apartment building had probably been too lazy to carry it all the way to a collection place and just left it where it was.

"It's almost brand new," Roland said, looking behind it for roaches.

Getting the washing machine back to my apartment was a lot of work. So was cleaning it up. We polished it until we could see our faces in it. Then, sweating and breathing heavily, we carried it into the kitchen and plugged it in. It worked!

The following evening Sotaro, my former Japanese teacher, came over.

"Why do people throw away usable things instead of giving them to someone else?" I asked, between beers.

"Well, to tell the truth," he said, lowering his voice, "old things might be full of bad spirits."

I was surprised to hear that and wanted to know more, but the conversation stopped. We began a whisky drinking competition, trying to see if we could guess the brand without looking at the label. Five hours later Sotaro left, walking in wide circles. I crawled to my bed.

古いモノには悪霊が宿るなんて迷信だよね？

I was dreaming of beautiful girls in small bikinis when a strange noise woke me up. Babies crying under a blanket? I turned on the lights and looked at the clock. 4:00 a.m. I must have been dreaming, I told myself, and turned off the lights.

But I heard the strange sound again. This time I was awake. I remembered what Sotaro had said. Had I brought unfriendly ghosts into my apartment? I sat up in bed and looked nervously around the room, half-expecting to see giant shadows jump out at me.

Then I heard a new sound. Something was scratching at my window! I'll never forget that moment of terror. I couldn't move. I kept looking at the window and pulled the curtains apart.

There, right in front of me, was a pair of angry, green, cat-like eyes floating in the air. I screamed and jumped back. The eyes disappeared.

The next morning I felt better. How silly of me! I thought. Ghosts! Ha! I just drank too much whiskey, that's all.

But just as I was leaving for work, I heard the same strange sounds again. Come on, I told myself. There's no such thing as ghosts.

I went over to the washing machine. The sounds were coming from behind it. I pushed it away from the wall and, to my great surprise, two kittens walked out. Feeling much better, I carried them outside. From out of nowhere, a big black cat appeared.

It caught the kittens in its mouth and ran away. Smiling to myself for being so silly, I turned to go back in.

"Excuse me, sir!" said a voice behind me. It was a policeman. "Have you seen a black washing machine, by any chance? The Tanaka family came to our police box two days ago. It seems that someone stole their washing machine. Any ideas?"

No one helped me carry the washing machine back to the Tanakas. No one stood by my side while I apologized to a stone-faced Mr. Tanaka. He didn't believe my story. In fact he got quite angry when I told him that I had thought his washing machine was junk.

Several months passed before I could walk around my neighborhood without people pointing at me. Now, a year later, almost everybody has forgotten about my little mistake.

But I'm still very angry at the Tanakas. They never thanked me for polishing their washing machine.

OL Ways

すごすぎる存在感、
OLは社内最強の味方か敵か?

ニッポン株式会社が世界に誇る存在、その名はOL。
怖いものなしで職場を闊歩し、アフター・ファイブを生き生きと過ごす
彼女たちをうらやましくも思うボルガさん。
それに社内で知りたいことがあれば、
管理職よりかはOLたちに聞くのが正解!
でもそんなボルガさんにとって、OLはときに怖い存在でもあるようです。

"I wish I was a woman," I told Makoto as a group of office ladies entered the office laughing.

"Are you planning to become a sort of *kabuki onnagata*?" Makoto asked with surprise.

"No, but after being at a Japanese company for a while, I have discovered something. Despite having few options for career development, women also have lots of advantages and incredible power," I began.

"For example: As soon as they get to the office they go into a changing room. They go there to update themselves on the latest developments around the office from the previous day. Over the years, I've learned that if I want good information on the company, I should ask an OL instead of a manager. I don't understand why stock analysts don't consult them when making reports on companies."

I continued, "They are only at the office from nine to five, and they stop working at mid-morning and mid-afternoon supposedly to prepare tea. At other hours of the day they also go to the washroom to smoke. All these breaks give them plenty of time to exchange information about the company."

OLのすごさ、その実態を語りだしたら止まらない！

As I progressed in my description, Makoto looked worried and tried to make sure no one else could hear us.

"They come to the office wearing brand-name clothing and change into sandals and uniforms. In New York, many women wear sneakers and change into dress shoes at the office. I have always wondered if these differences are related to the place where each expects to find a boyfriend."

Unfortunately, I have never been "targeted" in Japan and none of my own "targeting" has been successful. Perhaps it is because I also wear sandals at the office. I do wash my feet daily so...

"They talk all the time among themselves. If they cannot speak directly to their friends, they do so over the phone using very polite Japanese so no one will notice. Once, I told my boss that we should make them eat *gyoza*

with lots of garlic so they would keep their mouths shut," I said.

"There are different groups of OLs at the office. Each group eats together during lunchtime, leaves the office at the same time and travels abroad for holidays as a group. If you criticize one of them in front of the others, you risk getting sugar in your Japanese tea. And be happy if it is only sugar..."

OLさんを敵にするのも味方にするのも、どちらも大変！

I was getting enthusiastic, but before I could continue, Makoto said that he had some urgent business to do. He then quickly rushed out of the room. I immediately moved closer to Hiroshi's desk and told him exactly what I had told Makoto.

Then I added: "An OL has different voices. A very fast high-pitched one to make her sound very young and polite on the telephone. Another voice shows some nervousness because this is used when asking the boss for a salary increase or days off to go to Hawaii. This same voice becomes frightening if the boss keeps asking for tea. Finally, the last voice is the one used for talking with friends. I cannot believe all these voices belong to one person!"

As I spoke, Hiroshi began to stare at the area right above my shoulders, his eyes wide open with a scared look on his face. I suddenly realized that Mari was standing right behind me.

"What is that you're saying, Fun?" she asked. My face reddened. I had to think of something nice to say or else...

"I was telling Hiroshi that I don't agree with all those lies people tell about OLs. In my personal opinion, I think that OLs are incredibly nice. Especially when, after a long and busy day, they come to my desk and massage my shoulders."

Mari did not look very convinced, but she accepted my explanation.

Since then, I have become quite popular with the OLs. Unfortunately, I always end up surrounded by five women drinking like fish and talking only to each other— and I always end up having to pay the bill at the end of the evening.

Surviving at the Office

日本の会社で生き残るための処世術！

ある日突然、「日本の会社についてどう思うか？」、
と上司に尋ねられたボルガさん。
狭いオフィス、冷房の効きすぎなどについて話し、
本題に触れることを避けたあたり、もうかなり日本のサラリーマン的に？！
でも、やっぱり仕事の進め方や
上司の滅私奉公とも思える仕事ぶりは、
何年いっしょに働いても理解しがたいようです。

Mr. Tanaka, a manager from the general affairs department, strolled into our office. When I saw him getting closer, I quickly hid the comic book I was reading under some papers. It was 6:30 p.m., and I had finished my work for the day. I was killing time, waiting for the other guys to go home and trying to add some extra hours to my timecard. "What do you think of Japanese offices?" he asked.

"The other day I read a report from the Prime Minister's Office," I answered, trying to sound confident. "According to the statistics there are a lot of complaints. For example, 59.5 percent of the people think that offices are too small. Air-conditioning received complaints from

45.2 percent of the people," I said with authority, but a little afraid.

"I see. But what do YOU think?" he insisted.

上司からの尋問が始まった…リストラ策の第一歩？

I didn't want to give straight answers because I wasn't sure about Mr. Tanaka's intentions. I had heard that the company was planning on reducing the number of staff. Perhaps he was thinking about firing those who complained.

"Well, sometimes the office is too cold in summer," I began to say.

"What do you mean cold?" he interrupted looking at me over his eyeglasses.

"Well, it's not my opinion. Our OLs are always complaining and they have to bring blankets to the office every day to cover their legs. I love cool places," I lied, remembering the bad cold I had caught last summer. I was tempted to tell him about rooms being very hot in winter, but I thought it would be better to keep my opinions to myself.

"I see," he said, taking notes in his notebook. He asked if the OLs who complained were still at the office, but I told him they had already left. "By the way, are you busy now? Aren't you killing time?" he asked staring at my almost empty desk.

"Oh, no. I'm very busy...uh, I'm thinking of a new marketing campaign." I said. After many years in Japan I have learned that you must always say that you're busy, no matter what.

噴き出てきた本音、日本人上司への不満たらたら…

Mr. Tanaka grunted and walked away. I felt relieved, but his questions made me think about all my complaints about the office. Basically I agree with the statistics, although I would like to add that Japanese offices have too many papers, so people are always hidden behind piles of papers and books. Where are all those computers Japanese companies produce every year? Or is it a trick to sleep without being seen by the boss?

But if we are talking about complaints, there is one area of the office, which is usually ignored by the statistics: the boss. After many years of carefully observing and suffering in a Japanese office, I have reached the conclusion that the main differences between my boss and me, are as follows: When it takes me too long to finish a job, I'm too slow, I'm trying to steal the company's money by getting too much overtime, or I'm simply stupid. When my boss takes too long to finish a job, he is only being careful.

When I don't do a job, I'm lazy, but when he doesn't do a job it's because he's too busy.

When I stay at home because I have a cold, I must be lying and he calls me every two hours to make sure I'm

at my apartment. When he stays at home, he must be very ill, perhaps close to death.

When I drink too much, I'm a drunk, but when he drinks too much, he's only trying his best so that everybody has a good time.

When I spend some time outside the office, I must be wasting my time at a department store or chasing girls. When he spends time outside the office, he must be visiting a customer. And if he stays a long time it is because many people at the customer's office wanted to talk with him.

When I do something right, it's because the boss taught me, but when he does something right it's because he's perfect.

I have many more complaints, but I'm sure that more than hearing them from me, you'd like to add your own observations to the list. Oh—before I forget—don't tell my boss I wrote these things about him. He's the best person I've met in my whole life.

Red in the Face

日本人女性好みの
ルックスに挑戦!

日本では、外国人男性はモテル、ってよく言われるけれど、
最近ますますモテなくなったと感じるボルガさん。
そこで大学時代の友人にすすめられるままに、
人気ショップのカリスマ店員に
女の子をデートに誘うコツを尋ねに行きました。
やっともらえたアドバイスどおりにするために悪戦苦闘するボルガさん。
やっと準備はできたものの…

"For some reason it's becoming more difficult to find young women who want to date me," I told Makoto, a friend from my university days.

"Perhaps the problem is that you've been girl-hunting at the same place too long," Makoto said.

"You mean the company? But, that's a good place. Everybody knows me there," I said, defending my choice of a hunting ground.

"That's the reason no one wants to date you! Find someone who doesn't know you!" Makoto remarked.

I decided to take his advice and start meeting young women on the streets of Shibuya. I wore my most fashionable clothes and brightest smile, and rode the subway with high hopes.

"Go away!" said the first young woman I approached when I asked her to go out with me.

"Not now, not ever!" said another one that I invited to karaoke. She even tried to hit me with her portable phone. And that was only the beginning. After hours of walking the streets approaching young women with different nice invitations, I had sore feet and no date. I also noticed that there seemed to be very few girls that looked Japanese anymore. Most of the girls I talked to that day had light brown hair and very tanned faces. There were some girls who even had blond hair. I wondered what happened to the traditional beauties of

Japan—the ones I liked the most, with white faces and black hair. Was I getting too old?

日本の若い女の子好みのルックスに挑戦！

Makoto suggested I get advice from someone called a "charisma *ten-in*." He said it was a shop person who is popular and gives advice on fashion. I went to meet her in her shop. Her face was very tanned and she wore a very short skirt. "Excuse me. I need your advice on how to date Shibuya girls," I said humbly. She ignored me and continued to arrange clothes on a stand. "Please," I pleaded again. She wouldn't answer me. She probably thought I was hopeless.

Only after I kept begging her for hours, she finally answered. "Your hair is the wrong color, and what's worse, your face is too red. You need a tan." I thought she expected too much, but she was a charisma *ten-in*. Her advice, Makoto said, was very important.

After that, I went to a hair salon and had my hair dyed light brown. I wasn't very happy with my new image, but at this point, I'd do anything to get a date. The most important step was very difficult: I had to change the color of my face. I went to a tanning salon. I wanted to be tanned as soon as possible. The attendant suggested the "speedy course" and made me sit under a strong lamp. I felt like *yakitori* that was being roasted very slowly and expected someone to pour soy sauce on my face at any moment.

"You're finished. Come back in two days for another session," the attendant said after two hours of treatment. I wasn't very happy with the results: My face was as red as a lobster. "Don't worry," the attendant promised, "in two days it will turn into a nice tan."

はやりのルックスにしてみたけれど…

"Did you have an accident?" asked my boss, when he saw my face the next day at the office. My face became even redder from embarrassment. I decided to skip my next session at the tanning salon. Four days later I felt better, but was sad because the color of my face had returned to its usual red color.

"I suggest our extra speedy course," the attendant at the salon said confidently, "but you'll have to stay five hours under the lamp." After two hours I couldn't stand the lamp anymore. From the salon I took a taxi directly to a hospital.

Four weeks passed before my face had completely recovered. I wouldn't give up, though. I decided that make-up was the solution. I put a thick layer of a dark foundation on my face and left for Shibuya.

"No!" said the first girl I approached before running away as fast as she could.

The same thing happened with all the other girls I approached that day. "You look strange," said the last one, pointing at my face. I then realized that the make-up, mixed with my natural color, made me look like a carrot.

Now I'm back dating girls at the company again. To my surprise, they like my light brown hair. Hopefully red faces will become fashionable too.

A Perfect Salad

日本語を話せるのは
日本人だけではありません！

日本に何年か住んでいて、日本語もかなり上達したボルガさん。
でも、やはり電話での会話は、まだ時々難しいことも。
あるとき、デリバリーのピザを電話で注文しようとして会話が大混乱。
外国人だと日本語ができない、という
日本人の先入観もあるようです。
そこでモノは試しあれ、と日本名を名乗ってみることにしましたが…

After years in Japan, I've only just realized that I'm part of a big unfinished salad," I said, drinking a sip from my coffee. "You mean to say that you've turned into a vegetarian?" asked Kimiko, a long-time friend who was having a bite to eat with me after work. "Nope. I mean what I said. I'M PART of a salad," I said. Kimiko stared at me in disbelief.

"No, let me explain. It all started when I was able to speak a little more than restaurant Japanese. I could..." "Restaurant Japanese?" Kimiko interrupted. "That's when my language ability was limited to *kore* (this) or *are* (that) when pointing at the food display by the door of a restaurant," I said. I used to grab a waiter or, sometimes a customer, by the arm and pull him out to the food display and point at what I wanted to eat. Sometimes, they didn't understand it and tried to run away from me. So I started weightlifting, so that I could continue my language studies.

As my language abilities improved, I began to ask for dishes not shown in the displays...and it wasn't miso soup with rice all the time. For sure, my Japanese was worse than that of a five-year-old kid. But I thought I was ready to talk over the phone.

外国人の話す日本語って、そんなにわかりにくい？

Once I tried calling a pizza place. "Thank you for calling. This is Romanachi's pizza," I guessed someone said in fast Japanese. "I want to order a pizza," I said shyly. "Yes sir," the guy answered politely. "I was very happy. He had understood my Japanese." "Come on Fun, even if you had spoken Swahili the guy would have guessed that much," Kimiko interrupted again, laughing. "No one calls a pizza delivery shop except to order a pizza."

I ignored her. Her comments often hurt my feelings. "Your telephone number and address?" the pizza guy then asked. I tried to give him my number and address.

"Your name please?" he repeated. "My name is Fun," I replied in Japanese. "What was that?" he asked. "F-u-n," I spelled out as slowly as possible. "Oh! Ham, now I understand. You want ham on your pizza," the guy said.

"Very interesting. But what does all that have to do with you being part of an unfinished salad?" Kimiko said. "Well, I have a friend called Rimann. They always mistake his name for Piman (sweet pepper). We only need to meet someone called Tomato. The three of us will make a combination salad." I said, laughing at my own joke.

Kimiko's bored face disappointed me once again, but anyway I tried to explain that that phone call was the beginning of ongoing trouble. No one ever understood my name over the phone. Once I tried to buy tickets for a concert. When I gave my name, the receptionist started laughing. She didn't, or couldn't, stop—even for a little while. Then the girl began to cough as if something was stuck in her throat, so I hung up the phone.

日本名を名乗れば、問題解決と思いきや…

As time passed, I understood that sometimes it is difficult for Japanese people to understand foreigners' names. Then I started saying "My name is Tanaka," on the phone. That kept everybody happy. However, I have had some problems with this change of name. One day I ordered some *udon*. More than one hour passed and I didn't get my *udon*. I called to complain.

"The delivery boy went to the address you told us, but he couldn't find any Tanaka living there," a woman said. I explained that Tanaka lived at the same address. When I finally got the *udon* it was too cold to eat. I threw it away. The following day I added the name "Tanaka" to my nameplate by the door. No more problems with *udon* guys, I thought.

The next Sunday morning the bell rang very early. It was the apartment owner. She didn't look friendly. "Where's Miss Tanaka?" she asked. "I know your girlfriend is here with you. According to the contract only one person can live in this apartment," she said angrily, pushing past me into my room. Of course, she didn't find any girl. "Fun and Tanaka are the same person," I tried to explain. But I wasn't successful. She even checked in the closet and under the *kotatsu*. It took a two-hour-long explanation and, of course, I had to bring some presents before she would believe me.

Now I still use the Tanaka name sometimes. Often, people say that I don't look like a Tanaka. "I was adopted by a kind, *udon*-eating Japanese family," I tell them.

The Fortune of My Love

占いに自分の恋愛を 賭けられる?

お見合いで、履歴書交換だけで断られてしまったボルガさん。
理由は、動物占いによる相性が悪いから、ということでした。
がっかりしたけれど、占い人気に乗じて
女の子をデートに誘うことにしました。
自分で編み出した寿司占い、とちょっと凝ってみたものの、
やはりうまくいきません。
そこで、まずは自分の恋愛運を占ってもらうことにしました。

"Fun, here's the woman of your dreams." A couple of years ago, Mr. Yamamoto, the manager at my company, told me the personal history of a pretty woman. She had been introduced to him through the friend of an uncle of his wife's third cousin.

I carefully read her personal history and learned that she was into animal fortune-telling. I sent her the history of my life, clearly stating that I was born a rabbit, and like a rabbit, I was cute, intelligent, and fast to grab opportunities.

"She studied your career path at the company and decided that you should have been born a cat," Mr. Yamamoto said sadly, one week later. "According to the legend, the cat didn't get there in time when the gods assigned the twelve animals of the Chinese zodiac." The woman had rejected me without even meeting me. That night I walked home, lonely and desperate, until I realized that fortune-telling could be an interesting excuse to meet girls.

That week I invited Kimiko, a cute girl who came to our office to deliver an envelope, to eat sushi. "I'm an expert in sushi fortune-telling," I whispered to her. Surprisingly she agreed to come with me. How come she accepted my invitation after so many women had rejected me? Did she have hidden intentions? I put aside my worries. I wanted everything to be perfect. We met at a beautiful (and expensive) sushi restaurant in Roppongi. The president of my company had taken me there once before. "*Tako*, *ika* and *tai* for me," I ordered from the sushi master. "*Uni*, *ikura* and *sake*," Kimiko asked. We began to eat and talk.

寿司占いで女の子を口説こうとしたけれど…

"We've made a good start," I told her. "*Tai* and *sake*, white and pink, make a great combination and are easy to mix," I went on, just to impress Kimiko with my sushi fortune-telling. I talked a lot, drank green tea, and ate lots of free ginger. Kimiko barely said a word and kept eating the most expensive sushi cuts. My hair was beginning to turn green from the tea. When she said she had eaten enough, I asked for the bill.

"Seventy-thousand yen!!" I screamed, and wondered if they were trying to sell me the restaurant in installments. But I paid it like a gentleman, thinking about all the overtime I would have to work to make that much money.

"I had a great time talking to you," I said romantically. "The fish was delicious," Kimiko replied, staring at the ceiling. "Shall we meet again?" I asked. "My fortune-teller told me that *tai* and green tea make for a bad combination. It reflects a weak personality and a poor future," Kimiko replied. So I decided to go back to basic fortune-telling this time. After watching a movie in Ginza one night, I noticed a couple of middle-aged men sitting in front of tiny desks, holding young girls' hands. "What? The Japanese police lets them do that in the streets?" I asked my friend Makoto, still holding a can of beer. "No, Fun, they are looking at those girls' palms to see their future," he replied.

手相占いによる運命の女性と出会ってみたら…

The next day I was standing in a long line waiting for my turn. After half an hour, when I could hardly feel my legs anymore, finally "Mother of Ginza" told me to sit down. "What do you want to know?" she asked me. "I want to know what I have to do to get a nice girl," I answered.

"OK, roll the dice," she said, handing me some plastic dice. "Excuse me?" "Just roll, come on!" The Mother of Ginza sounded like she was in a hurry, so I threw the dice right away. "Three, huh. OK, tomorrow get off at the station three stops away from where you live. Then you will meet a girl of your dreams," she said in confidence. I was a bit suspicious, but gave her 3,000 yen and left.

The next day I did what she told me. As I got off the train, a beautiful woman walked past me. She must have been in her mid-20s. As she walked down the stairs, her long black hair danced rhythmically on her shoulders. It was love at first sight. "Oh my god, the fortune-telling was real!" I thanked the Mother, and followed the woman all the way to her house. I checked the nameplate. It was the Yoshimoto family.

I asked the neighbors the name of the daughter of the Yoshimoto family. "Yumiko. She's gorgeous," they said. To me, her name had the sound of a small river flowing down a mountain in spring. I wrote a passionate love letter to Yumiko, stressing the fact that I could teach her English for free, and dropped it into her mailbox.

Three days later she knocked on my door. I admired her eyes shining beautifully in the sunlight. "We were very flattered by your letter, but..." she began to say. "But you won't accept a foreigner," I interrupted. "The age difference is too big," she said. "That shouldn't be a problem. And remember, I can teach English for free." I interrupted again. "Very generous of you. But Yumiko, our daughter, should learn Japanese first. She's only three months old. I'm her mother."

Before she left my door, I made her promise that she wouldn't tell anyone about my love letter.

巻末注釈

NOTES

　この本の英文はすべてやさしい英語で書かれていますが、中学・高校の検定教科書と過去3年間のセンター試験に含まれない単語と意味のわかりにくい表現を解説します。日本語訳は文中の意味に沿っています。

　その他にも、知っていると役立つこと、同意語や略語の説明も豊富に掲載しました。このNOTESだけでも読んでいると楽しく、勉強になります。ボルガさんのユーモアが、ことばづかいなどからも読みとれることでしょう！

"Domo Domo" Paradise

- **p.10** **immigration**:「出入国管理カウンター」。immigrateという単語には「移住する」という意味があります。
- **p.10** **though**:「でも、だが」。althoughとほぼ同じ意味の口語ですが、文尾や挿入的に使えるのはthoughのみです。
- **p.10** **guys**:「男、やつ」。ただし、複数の相手に対してyou guysと言うときは女性にも使います。口語。
- **p.10** **pick up**:「拾う」
- **p.10** **on the way out**:「出る途中で」
- **p.11** **handy**:「便利な、使いやすい」
- **p.11** **dormitory**:「寮」。省略してdormと言われることもよくあります。
- **p.11** **bla bla**:「何とか何とか」。あまり意味のないことをクダクダと話している様子や、聞き取れなかった部分を表すときに使われる表現です。
- **p.11** **impossible-to-understand**:「理解不能な」。くだけた表現ではしばしば、whichなどを使わず単語を「-」でつないで形容詞的な使い方をします。
- **p.12** **unrecognizable**:「聞き分けのつかない」
- **p.12** **congratulate**:「祝う」
- **p.12** **outstanding**:「傑出した」
- **p.12** **kind of**:「ちょっと」。同じ意味でsort ofという表現もよく使われます。
- **p.12** **on time**:「時間通り」。この場合は「日本人は大抵、時間を守るのではなかったのか」という意味になります。
- **p.12** **turn up**:「現れる」。この場合、appearと同じ意味です。
- **p.12** **wave**:「手を振る」
- **p.12** **confuse**:「混乱する」
- **p.15** **run into ...**:「～に衝突する」。他にも、「～にばったり出くわす」という意味でよく使われる表現です。
- **p.15** **crash**:「衝突」
- **p.15** **knock ... to the floor**:「～にぶつかり床に倒す」
- **p.15** **ever**:「決して」。このように否定文で使われる場合は強調の意味になります。
- **p.16** **seldom ...**:「めったに～ない」。Hardlyやscarcelyも同じ意味です。
- **p.16** **far from perfect**:「完璧というには程遠い」
- **p.17** **rude**:「無作法な」
- **p.17** **a copy of ...**:「～1部」。記事を数える場合はcopyを使います。

To Eat, or Not to Eat

- **p.19** **To eat, or not to eat**：「食うべきか食わぬべきか」。シェイクスピアの『ハムレット』に登場する有名な台詞 "To be or not to be, that is the question." (生きるべきか死すべきか、それが問題だ) をもじったタイトルです。
- **p.20** **task**：「務め」。厄介な仕事や意に反して課せられた任務などを指します。
- **p.20** **Let me explain myself better.**：「もっときちんと説明させてください」。explain oneself には、自分の不始末などについて弁明する、あるいは自分の言いたいことをはっきりさせる、などの意味があります。
- **p.20** **afford to …**：「〜する余裕がある」。経済的余裕に関して使われることが多い言葉です。
- **p.21** **to tell you the truth**：「本当のことを言うと」
- **p.21** **tasteless**：「味がない」。ほかにも「趣味が悪い」などの意味があります。
- **p.21** **mayonnaise**：「マヨネーズ」
- **p.21** **rubber**：「ゴム」
- **p.21** **convince**：「納得させる」
- **p.21** **note**：「注意する」。このような場合は「心に留めておいてください」という意味になります。
- **p.22** **love at first sight**：「一目惚れ」
- **p.22** **extra**：「余計な」。extra large (特大サイズ) など、「特別な」という意味もあります。
- **p.23** **form**：「形態」。動詞としては「作り上げる」などの意味があります。
- **p.24** **occasion**：「場合」。「機会」という意味もあります。
- **p.24** **invite … out**：「…を外食に招待する」。この場合のように、out は文脈によって「外食に」という意味を持つこともあります。
- **p.24** **aquarium**：「水槽」。「水族館」という意味もあります。
- **p.24** **show … to …**：「…を〜に案内する」
- **p.25** **mosquito**：「蚊」
- **p.25** **experienced**：「経験豊富な」
- **p.25** **the next**：the next moment の略
- **p.26** **manage to …**：「どうにか〜する」
- **p.27** **drinking the soup**：「スープを飲む」。皿からスプーンで飲む場合は drink ではなく eat を使います。
- **p.27** **nicely**：「上品に」、「ちゃんと」

Talk to Me, Please

- **p.30** **similarly**:「同様に」
- **p.31** **refuse**:「辞退する」。「拒否する」などの意味もあります。名詞形は refusal です。
- **p.31** **OLs**:OLという言葉は和製英語なので、使い方には注意しましょう。
- **p.31** **from … on**:「〜以来」
- **p.32** **over and over**:「何度も何度も繰り返して」。again and again も同じ意味です。
- **p.32** **besides**:「その上」。会話でよく使われる表現ですが、文章やかしこまった場では furthermore や moreover などが使われます。
- **p.32** **around**:「周りに」
- **p.32** **go further**:「もっと先に行く」。further は far の比較級で、この場合は「それ以上の会話になることはなかった」という意味になります。
- **p.33** **prefecture**:「県」
- **p.34** **wonders of nature**:「自然の不思議」
- **p.34** **care about …**:「〜に構う」。ほかにも「関心を持つ」あるいは「心配する」などの意味があります。
- **p.34** **arrange a date**:「デートの約束を取り付ける」。文脈によっては「日取りを決める」という意味になります。
- **p.34** **give a thought to …**:「〜を考える」。「〜を考慮する」という意味もあります。
- **p.34** **turn one's eyes to the ground**:「〜が視線を地面に向ける」
- **p.35** **bookish**:「堅苦しい」。自然な会話ではなく、本に出てくるような硬い感じの、という意味です。
- **p.35** **"Tarzan" language**:「ターザンの言葉」。つまり、単純で原始的な話し方という意味です。
- **p.35** **put up with**:「我慢する」
- **p.35** **barber shop**:「床屋」
- **p.36** **after all**:「結局」
- **p.36** **ever since …**「〜以来」。ever は since を強調しています。
- **p.36** **all**:「完全に」
- **p.36** **saying**:「発言」。saying には、ほかにも「ことわざ」という意味があります。

Renting a Piece of Tokyo

- **p.38 in line**:「列をなして」
- **p.39 carry on**:「続ける」
- **p.39 real estate agent**:「不動産屋」
- **p.39 big name**:「有名どころ」。人について「有名人」という意味で使われることが多い表現です。
- **p.39 advertisement**:「広告」。動詞のadvertiseは「宣伝する」という意味です。
- **p.39 mid-twenties**:「20代半ば」。年齢だけでなく、時代についても「○○年代」という意味で使われます。
- **p.39 greet**:「挨拶する」。「迎える」などの意味もあります。
- **p.39 housing**:「住宅」、「住宅計画」
- **p.40 broad smile**:「満面の微笑み」
- **p.40 catch one's attention**:「~の注意を引く」
- **p.41 sign a contract**:「契約書にサインする」
- **p.41 cough**:「咳をする」。この単語のghはfの音で発音されます。
- **p.41 a wild idea**:「突拍子もない考え」
- **p.41 somewhat**:「いくらか」
- **p.41 budget**:「予算」
- **p.41 don't bother with**:「相手にしない」。他動詞の場合、通常否定形で「気にかけない」という意味で使われます。
- **p.41 assistance**:「支援」。この場合は「手助けを申し出てくれた」という意味になります。
- **p.41 father-in-law**:「義父」。同様にmother-in-lawは「義母」、sister-in-lawは「義姉」で、姻戚をまとめてin-lawsと言います。
- **p.42 stand**:「耐える」。同じ意味でbearもよく使われます。
- **p.42 cockroach**:「ゴキブリ」。後に出てくるroachはcockroachの略で、同じ意味です。
- **p.43 five-story**:「5階建ての」。建物の5階はfifth floorです。アメリカでは1階をfirst floorと言い、イギリスでは1階(地階)をground floor、2階をfirst floorと呼ぶことが多いので、注意が必要です。
- **p.44 landlady**:「(女性の)大家さん」。女性の地主を指すこともあります。男性の場合はlandlordを使います。
- **p.44 avoid**:「避ける」
- **p.44 quite a few**:「かなりの数の」

P.47 ➡ P.53

Train Shock

- **p.48** **pick up**:「迎えに行く」。ほかにも「拾う」という意味があります。
- **p.48** **rather**:「かなり」
- **p.48** **supposed to …**:「〜するはず」。suppose には「仮定する」や「想定する」という意味があります。
- **p.49** **major**:「大きな」。「ものすごい〜」という意味でよく使われる口語表現です。このすぐ後に出てくる major city の major は「主要な」という意味です。
- **p.49** **earthquake**:「地震」
- **p.49** **pusher**:「押す人」。動詞の末尾に er が付くと、その動作をする人や物を指します。
- **p.49** **something to talk about**:「話すに足ること」
- **p.49** **the other day**:「先日」。day の代わりに morning を入れて「この前の朝」という意味でも使われます。
- **p.49** **escape**:「逃げ出す」
- **p.50** **right**:「すっかり」。この right は強調の役割をしていて、この場合は「旗を見事に取り上げた」という意味になります。
- **p.50** **hips**:「腰」。このように複数形で使われることが多い単語です。
- **p.50** **dirty**:「いやらしい」。「汚い」や「卑猥な」という意味があります。
- **p.50** **in silence**:「静かに」。silently と同じ意味です。
- **p.50** **conclude**:「結論する」
- **p.50** **make room**:「場所を作る」
- **p.50** **pass by**:「通り過ぎる」
- **p.51** **poor**:「かわいそうな」。人について使う場合、ほかに「貧乏な」という意味があります。
- **p.52** **bullet train**:「超特急電車」。日本で bullet train という場合は新幹線を指します。
- **p.52** **over one's shoulder**:「〜の肩越しに」
- **p.53** **with no luck**:「ツキがない」。この場合は「探したけれど、見つからなかった」という意味になります。
- **p.53** **drunk**:「酔っ払い」
- **p.53** **knock**:「叩く」。この場合はサーフ・ボードが周りの人の頭にぶつかるという状況です。
- **p.53** **Write soon.**:「返事を待っています」。親しい人への手紙の最後によく使う表現で、「早く返事をください」という意味です。

Sweet Melodies of Love

- **p.56** **catch one's eye**:「目をとらえる」。She caught my eye. で、「彼女のことが目に留まった」という風に訳すこともできます。
- **p.56** **get one's attention**:「注意を引く」。「〜に対して注意を払う」は pay attention to ...。
- **p.56** **dormitory**:「寮」。友人同士の会話などでは、短縮形の dorm が使われることも多く見られます。
- **p.56** **serenade**:「セレナーデ」
- **p.57** **beloved**:「最愛の人」
- **p.57** **the following night**:「その次の夜」
- **p.57** **noise**:「騒音、雑音」。単なる「音」である sound に対して、noise は余計なもの、という意味を含むので、本文でボルガさんが気分を害しているわけです。
- **p.57** **down there**:「そちら」という意味ですが、down をつけることによって、「(下のほうの)そちら」と、場所がわからない中でも具体化することができます。上のほうを指す場合は up there と言います。
- **p.58** **bucket**:「バケツ」
- **p.58** **bother**:「迷惑をかける、じゃまする」。お願いなどをする際に丁寧な言い出し方として、I'm sorry to bother you, but... (「お邪魔してしまってごめんなさい、でも〜」) などがあります。
- **p.59** **backwards**:「後ろに、後方に」
- **p.59** **fell**: fall の過去形。この場合は「転んだ」という意味。
- **p.59** **ouch!**:「痛い!」。他に That hurts! のような言い方もあります。
- **p.59** **spoil**:「だめにする」。また、a spoiled kid (「甘やかされた子供」) のように「(一般的に子供を)甘やかす」という意味もあります。
- **p.59** **cactus**:「サボテン」
- **p.59** **rear**:「お尻」
- **p.59** **sympathetically**:「同情して」
- **p.60** **next-door**:「隣の家の、隣に住む」
- **p.60** **wreck**:「壊す」

P.61 ➡ P.70

Osaka in White

- **p.62** **over the phone**:「電話越しに」
- **p.62** **some time ago**:「しばらく前」
- **p.62** **think it over**:「それについてよく考える」
- **p.62** **in advance**:「あらかじめ」。この場合は「3週間前に」という意味です。
- **p.63** **refrigerator**:「冷蔵庫」。冷凍庫は freezer です。
- **p.63** **fill out**:「記入する」。fill in も似た意味で使われることがあります。
- **p.63** **Catholic**:「(キリスト教)カトリックの」
- **p.63** **mass**:「ミサ」(カトリック教会の礼拝)
- **p.64** **making a lot of noise**:「大きな音を立てて」。アメリカなどでは、新婚夫婦は挙式後や新婚旅行の際に飾り立てた自動車の後ろに紐でいくつもの空き缶をつなぎ、それを引きずって大きな音を立てながら移動する慣習があります。
- **p.64** **waltz**:「ワルツ」
- **p.64** **much**:「とても」。この場合は very や so と同じ意味です。
- **p.64** **the big day**:「大事な日」。この場合はサチコの結婚式を指します。
- **p.66** **in great detail**:「非常に詳しく」
- **p.66** **since ...**:「〜だったので」。このような場合は、because と同じ意味です。
- **p.66** **loudspeaker**:「拡声器」。loudspeaker は speaker と省略することもあります。
- **p.69** **You know — after the kombu.**:「わかりますよね、あの昆布の後だったことだし」。つまり、早くケーキを食べて不味かった昆布の口直しをしたかった、ということです。この場合の you know は、その後の言葉を強調するための前置きです。
- **p.69** **in fact**:「それどころか実際には」
- **p.70** **could not help ...**:「〜をせざるを得なかった」
- **p.70** **frosting**:「糖衣」(ケーキなどをカラフルに覆う砂糖菓子)
- **p.70** **in a second**:「その瞬間」
- **p.70** **it was all over ...**:「それは〜まみれになっていた」
- **p.70** **scream**:「金切り声を上げる」

Meetings and More Meetings

- **p.74** **no matter ...**:「たとえ〜でも」。この場合は「たとえどんなに長くこの国にいても」という意味になります。
- **p.74** **so far**:「これまでのところ」
- **p.74** **hold true**:「当てはまる」
- **p.74** **suffer**:「苦しむ」
- **p.74** **chat**:「おしゃべり」。インターネット用語の「チャット」もここから来ています。
- **p.74** **department**:「部署」。百貨店は department store です。
- **p.75** **present**:「出席している」。欠席していることは absent です。
- **p.75** **excuse**:「言い訳」
- **p.75** **were to have a meeting**:「会議を開くことになっていた」
- **p.75** **boring**:「退屈な」
- **p.75** **scold**:「叱る」
- **p.75** **Mind you**:「いいですか」。相手の注意を促すための挿入句です。
- **p.75** **beforehand**:「あらかじめ」
- **p.76** **there is a very good chance that ...**:「〜である可能性がとても高い」
- **p.76** **ZZZ**:「グーグー」。寝息の音です。
- **p.76** **UFLOs（Unidentified Flying Long Objects）**:UFO（Unidentified Flying Object＝未確認飛行物体）をもじった表現です。
- **p.76** **boutique**:「ブティック」。もともとフランス語から来た言葉で、発音するときは ti にアクセントを置きます。
- **p.77** **thanks to ...**:「〜のおかげで」。「〜のせいで」という意味になることもあります。
- **p.77** **spot**:「場所」
- **p.78** **come to think about ...**:「〜について考えてみると」
- **p.78** **catch up with ...**:「(不足している)〜を取り戻す」。睡眠だけでなく、勉強に追いつく、などという場合にも使われます。
- **p.78** **so as to ...**:「〜するために」
- **p.79** **entertaining**:「面白い」。この言葉は interesting などとは違い、楽しめる、というニュアンスです。

P.81 → P.88

Who Cares?

- **p.81** **Who cares?**:「構うものか」。「だから何?」といったニュアンスでよく使われる表現です。
- **p.82** **get ready to …**:「〜をする用意をする」
- **p.82** **give advice**:「助言をする」。動詞では advise です。
- **p.82** **well then**:「それじゃあ」
- **p.82** **make sense**:「道理にかなう」。この場合は「そんなの訳がわからないよ」というニュアンスです。
- **p.84** **fell open**:「ぽかんと開いた」。このような場合の fall は「落ちる」という意味ではなく、ある状態に陥ることを指します。
- **p.84** **un-Japanese**:「非日本的」。形容詞の前に un が付くとその逆の意味になります。
- **p.84** **corn flakes**:「コーンフレーク」。単数形では使わないので注意しましょう。snowflake は雪片を指します。
- **p.84** **fire**:「首にする」
- **p.85** **slap**:「叩く」。hit とは違い、平手で叩くことを指します。「背中を叩く」は slap on the back ですが、「顔を平手打ちする」という場合は slap in the face です。
- **p.85** **potted plant**:「鉢植え植物」
- **p.85** **tiring**:「疲れる」。疲れた状態は tired です。
- **p.86** **call in**:「呼び入れる」
- **p.86** **demand to …**:「〜したいと言って聞かない」。demand には「要求する」などの意味があります。
- **p.86** **suck**:「吸う」
- **p.86** **sure**:「そうですね」。返事として sure を使う場合、同意や許可の意味になります。
- **p.86** **whatever**:「何でもいいけど」。このような場合は「そんなことはどうでも良い」というニュアンスです。
- **p.87** **raw**:「生の」
- **p.87** **run out of …**:「〜を切らす」。この場合「もう聞くことがなくなった」という意味です。
- **p.87** **bandage**:「包帯」
- **p.88** **by itself**:「ひとりでに」。海外では、日本のようにタクシーのドアが自動で開くことはほとんどなく、これは初めて日本でタクシーに乗る外国人がよく驚くことのひとつです。

International Business

- **p.90** **on business**：「仕事で」
- **p.90** **PC**：「パソコン」。personal computerの略です。
- **p.90** **business trip**：「出張」
- **p.90** **manager**：「部局長」。いろいろな意味を持つ単語ですが、この場合のmy managerは「うちの部長」あるいは「うちの課長」といった意味です。
- **p.90** **interrupt**：「さえぎる」
- **p.91** **salaryman**：「サラリーマン」。和製英語なので注意しましょう。英語では会社員はbusinessmanです。
- **p.91** **mom**：「ママ」。男女や年齢を問わず、最も一般的な、母親の呼び方です。
- **p.91** **whisper**：「ささやく」
- **p.91** **keep quiet**：「静かにしている」
- **p.91** **mister**：「おじさん」。このような場合はsirと同様、男性に対する呼びかけの言葉です。
- **p.92** **Gimme!**：「ちょうだい！」Give me! の口語的な表記です。
- **p.92** **tender**：「細やかな」
- **p.92** **get tired of ...**：「～に飽きる」
- **p.92** **working overtime**：「残業すること」。名詞のovertimeは「残業」の意味です。
- **p.92** **make a good impression on ...**：「～に良い印象を与える」
- **p.93** **vice president**：「副社長」。vice chairpersonというと副議長を指します。
- **p.93** **familiar with**：「よく知っている」
- **p.93** **Down Under**：「オーストラリア（の別名）」
- **p.93** **mates**：「みんな」。オーストラリアで「友達」という意味でよく使われる言葉で、このように、あいさつなどの際の相手への呼びかけにもなります。
- **p.94** **lean**：「体を寄せる」。「寄りかかる」という意味もあります。
- **p.94** **in circles**：「円を描きながら」。酔って千鳥足の状態です。
- **p.95** **toothbrush**：「歯ブラシ」
- **p.95** **sideways**：「横向きに」。この場合、壁の方を向き、壁に沿ってカニ歩きのような状態で歩いたという意味になります。
- **p.96** **unsuccessful**：「不成功の」

A Dog in My Life

- **p.98 walk around**:「歩き回る」
- **p.98 to tell the truth**:「実を言うと」
- **p.98 feel like … ing**:「〜する気になる」、「〜したい」。I want to ... とほぼ同意です。
- **p.98 translator**:「翻訳家」。「通訳」は interpreter。
- **p.98 good for you**:「良かったね」、「良かったじゃないか」。状況がその人物にとって都合のいい、幸せな方向に変化した時にかけられるセリフ。
- **p.99 ugly-looking**:「ぶさいくな外見の」。反対に「外見がいい」ことを表す言葉・表現には handsome、good-looking などがあります。
- **p.99 juicy**:ここでは「肉汁の多い」という意味で使われています。
- **p.99 take … for a walk**:「〜を散歩に連れていく」。ちなみに take a walk は「散歩する」。
- **p.100 half-open**:「半開きで」。「全開」は full-open。
- **p.100 mess**:(姿・場所などが) めちゃくちゃな様
- **p.100 drunk**:「酔っ払い」。同じく drink から派生した言葉で drunkard もありますが、こちらは drunk よりも印象が悪く、「のんだくれ」のような意味です。
- **p.101 follow one's advice**:「〜のアドバイスに従う」
- **p.101 apologize**:「謝る」
- **p.101 sore**:「痛い」。喉が痛いときは I have a sore throat. と言います。
- **p.101 high-quality**:「質の高い」、「良質の」。反対は low-quality です。
- **p.101 grrrr**:犬の鳴き声「グルルルル」。他に「ワンワン」は bow-wow、猫の鳴き声で「ニャーニャー」は meow または mew、喉を鳴らす「ゴロゴロ」は purr、怒ってうなる声は spit と書きます。
- **p.101 unfriendly**:「不親切な、情のない」。反対語は friendly です。
- **p.101 dangerous look in one's eyes**:「危険な目つきで」。「やさしい目つきで」は、tender look in one's eyes。
- **p.102 plastic bag**:「ビニール袋」
- **p.102 terrific**:「素晴らしい」
- **p.102 a slice of ham**:「1枚のハム」。ハムを数えるときには slice を使います。a slice of pizza のように、他のものに使うことも。
- **p.102 salami**:「サラミソーセージ」

Lines into the Future

- **p.106 co-worker**:「同僚」。他にも、colleague、fellow worker など。
- **p.106 read one's hand**:「手相を見る」。hand の代わりに palm を使うこともあります。「手相」は palm reading、「手相見」は palmist。
- **p.106 fortune-telling**:「占い」。fortune は元来「運、幸運、富、財産」などの意味を持つ単語です。「占い師」は fortune-teller。
- **p.107 middle-aged**:「中年の」(大体40〜60歳程度の人に対して)。middle-ager は「中年の人」という意味で使われます。「若年」は young-aged、または young age です。
- **p.107 No way!**:「まさか！ 絶対ダメ！ ありえない！」などの意味で使われる口語表現です。同じような意味で、Get out of here! なども言うことがあります。
- **p.107 What about...?**:「〜はどうですか？」。カジュアルな表現です。
- **p.108 wonderfully**:「驚くべき、素晴らしい」
- **p.108 from that day on**:「その日からずっと」。この on は「続いていく」という意味で使われています。
- **p.108 bank account**:「銀行口座」。「口座を開く」は open an account。
- **p.108 second opinion**:現在では、病院で診察を受けるときなどにカタカナ日本語としてもよく聞くようになった「セカンド・オピニオン」。ひとりの意見だけではなく、なるべく多くの人に話を聞いて公平に正しい決断をしようという考えに基づいた言葉です。
- **p.109 tons of ...**:「たくさんの〜」。これもカジュアルな表現です。公的な場、ビジネスシーンなどではあまり使わないほうが良いでしょう。
- **p.110 see each other more often**:「もっと頻繁に会う」が直訳ですが、デートに誘うときのセリフとしてよく聞く表現です。

Night Hunter

- **p.112 washing machine**：「洗濯機」
- **p.112 you name it**：「何でもある」、「何でもあてはまる」という時に使う表現です。直訳すると「何でも言ってみなさい(それは全部あるから)」。
- **p.112 burnable**：「可燃性の」
- **p.112 embrrassing**：「恥ずかしい」
- **p.112 well before …**：「〜よりかなり前に」。ここでは well は余裕を持たせる意味で使われています。
- **p.112 high hope**：「高い望み」
- **p.113 brand new**：「まっさらの、まったくの新品で」
- **p.113 roach**：「ゴキブリ」 (=cockroach)
- **p.113 polish**：「磨く、つやを出す」
- **p.113 plug in**：「プラグを差し込む」
- **p.113 come over**：「(家に)やって来る」
- **p.114 between beers**：「ビールの間に」、つまり「ビールを飲みながら」の意。また、over a cup of coffee (「コーヒーを飲みながら」) のように over を使うのも一般的です。
- **p.114 crawl**：「はう、のろのろ行く」
- **p.114 bikinis**：「ビキニ」
- **p.114 sit up in bed**：「ベッドに座って」
- **p.115 terror**：「恐怖」
- **p.115 cat-like**：「猫のような」。この場合の like は「〜のような」という意味で使われています。ほかにも woman-like (「女性のような」)、teacher-like (「先生のような」) のように言うことができます。
- **p.115 How silly of me!**：「僕は何て馬鹿なんだ!」。このように「〜 of 人」の表現は「〈人〉はなんて〜(性格、状態)なんだろう」という意味でよく使われます。たとえば、It's really thoughtful of you. と言えば、「なんてあなたは優しいんでしょう」となります。
- **p.116 to one's great surprise**：「驚いたことには」
- **p.116 nowhere**：「どこにも」。この場合は、from out of nowhere で「どこからか」という意味になります。また、似た表現で anywhere (「どこでも」)、somewhere (「どこかで」) などがあります。
- **p.117 stone-faced**：「表情がない」

OL Ways

- **p.120 a sort of ...**:「一種の〜」。このほかに同じ意味でよく使われる表現として、a kind of 〜があります。
- **p.120 option**:「オプション、選択肢」
- **p.120 incredible**:「信じがたい、すごい」
- **p.120 update**:「最新のものにする、アップデートする」
- **p.120 analyst**:「分析者、アナリスト」。ここでは、stock analyst で「証券アナリスト」(株価などの動向を分析する専門家)。
- **p.120 supposedly**:「想像上、たぶん」。また、Supposingly...と文章を始める場合は、「〜と仮定して」という意味になります。
- **p.120 washroom**:「トイレ」。ほかの言い方として、rest room、bathroom などがあります。
- **p.121 brand-name**:「高級ブランドの」
- **p.121 sneakers**:「スニーカー」
- **p.121 unfortunately**:「残念ながら」
- **p.122 keep mouth shut**:「口を閉じる」、つまり「黙る」という意味です。ケンカの場面では Keep your mouth shut!(「黙ってろ!」)という表現を耳にしますが、これはかなり失礼な言葉です。
- **p.122 enthusiastic**:「熱狂的な」
- **p.122 frightening**:「恐るべき、驚くべき」
- **p.123 redden**:「顔を赤くする」。ほかに、I was blushed.と、blush も「顔を(恥ずかしさで)赤くする」という意味で使われます。
- **p.123 massage**:「マッサージをする」。名詞としても同じ単語を用います。
- **p.123 convince**:「納得させる」
- **p.123 end up ...**:「結局〜なる」。I always end up arguing with my mother. は、「結局いつも母親とケンカしてしまう」という意味。

Surviving at the Office

- **p.126 stroll**:「ぶらぶら歩く、散歩する」
- **p.126 kill time**:「時間をつぶす」
- **p.126 timecard**:「タイムカード」
- **p.126 Prime Minister**:「首相、総理大臣」
- **p.126 statistic**:「統計」
- **p.126 complaints**:「苦情、文句」
- **p.126 air-conditioning**:「エアコン」
- **p.127 intention**:「意図、意思、目的」。thought(「考え、思い」)などに比べて、より明確な目的を持っていることをあらわす単語です。
- **p.127 eyeglasses**:「メガネ」
- **p.127 be tempted to …**:「～したい誘惑に駆られる」。It's tempting.といえば、「あれは魅力的だ」という意味になります。
- **p.128 keep … to myself**:「～を自分の胸の内だけにしまっておく」
- **p.128 no matter what**:「たとえ何があろうと」。同じ意味で、whatever happensと言うこともできます。
- **p.128 grunt**:「ぶーぶー言う、不平を言う」
- **p.128 relieve**:「ほっとする、安堵する」。名詞のreliefを使うと、It's a relief.で、「ああ、安心した」となります。
- **p.128 piles of …**:「たくさんの～」
- **p.128 observe**:「注視する、観察する」
- **p.129 as follows**:「以下の通りです」。必ず、as followsのあとにコロン(:)を忘れず入れましょう。
- **p.129 overtime**:「残業、定時間以外の」

P.131 ➙ P.136

Red in the Face

- **p.132 remark**：「意見を述べる、留意する」
- **p.132 not ever**：「永遠にない」。同じような状況で相手に望みがないことを教える際には、In your dreams.（「夢の中でもなきゃ無理」）のような表現も使ったりしますが、どちらも非常にきつい印象を与えますので注意しましょう。
- **p.132 portable phone**：「携帯電話」。アメリカではこのほかに cellular phone、または略して cell phone というのが一般的です。また、イギリスでは mobile phone と呼ぶことのほうが多いようです。
- **p.133 charisma**：「カリスマ（人を信服させる強い特殊な能力）」
- **p.133 tanned**：「日焼けして」
- **p.133 humbly**：「謙遜して」
- **p.134 plead**：「懇願する、弁護する」
- **p.134 hopeless**：「望みのない、絶望的な」
- **p.134 what's worse**：「さらに悪いことには」。ほかに、what's even worse、to make things even worse という言い方もあります。
- **p.134 tan**：「日焼け」
- **p.134 a hair salon**：「美容室」。「床屋」は a barbarshop です。
- **p.134 speedy**：「敏速な、スピーディーな」
- **p.134 lamp**：「ランプ、明かり」
- **p.134 soy sauce**：「しょうゆ」
- **p.134 at any moment**：「いつでも」。同じ意味で、at anytime があります。
- **p.134 one is finished**：「〜は終わりだ」。絶望的な状況に陥った際に使う表現です。また、You're doomed.のように、doom を使っても同じ意味になります。
- **p.134 session**：「セッション、区切り」
- **p.135 embarrassment**：「恥ずかしさ、当惑」
- **p.136 make-up**：「化粧、メーキャップ」
- **p.136 hopefully**：「うまくいけば」。希望的観測を示す際に文頭に置くことが多い単語です。

A Perfect Salad

- **p.138 sip**:「ひと口、ひと吸い」
- **p.138 vegetarian**:「ベジタリアン、菜食主義者」。宗教やポリシーなどの理由によって日本以外の国ではしばしばベジタリアンの方々を見かけます。
- **p.138 long-time**:「長年の」
- **p.138 nope**:「いいえ(no)」が口語表現として変化したもので、カジュアルな会話、おどけて話すときなどに使います。「はい(yes)」の場合、yepが口語表現として使われることがあります。
- **p.138 weightlifting**:「重量上げ、ウェートトレーニング」
- **p.140 spell out**:「一字一字書く」
- **p.141 ongoing**:「進行中の」
- **p.141 receptionist**:「受付、応接係」
- **p.141 as if...**:「まるで〜のように」。同じ意味でlikeを使うこともあります。友人同士の会話でいやみを言うときなどにas ifから文章を始めて言うこともあります。As if you care about my problem!は「私の問題なんてどうせ気にしてないんでしょうよ」という意味になります。
- **p.142 contract**:「契約」
- **p.142 angrily**:「怒って、憤慨して」
- **p.142 adopt**:「養子にする」

The Fortune of My Love

- **p.144 woman of one's dreams**：「夢にまで見た女性」。your dream woman と言うこともできます。
- **p.144 be into ...**：「〜に夢中」
- **p.144 career path**：「キャリアの道、キャリアパス」
- **p.144 assign**：「命じる、指定する」
- **p.144 Chinese zodiac**：「干支」
- **p.144 desperate**：「絶望的な、やけの」
- **p.144 How come ... ?**：「なぜ〜？」。why と同じ意味ですが、その後は疑問詞の場合と異なり、肯定文と同じ順序で文章を続けますので、注意しましょう。
- **p.144 put aside**：「〜をわきへやる、無視する」
- **p.145 ginger**：「しょうが」。この場合は寿司屋の紅しょうがを指しています。
- **p.145 barely**：「ほとんど〜ない」。hardly の同義語です。
- **p.146 in installments**：「分割払いで」。installment sale は「割賦販売」のことです。
- **p.146 romantically**：「ロマンチックに」
- **p.147 dice**：「さいころ」。「振る」という動詞には roll を使います。
- **p.148 rhythmically**：「リズミカルに、調子よく」
- **p.148 love at first sight**：「最初の出会いで好きになる」、つまり「一目ぼれ」のことです。
- **p.148 gorgeous**：「ゴージャスな、豪華な、すばらしい」。人に対しては、たいてい相当美しい外見を持っているときに使います。
- **p.149 passionate**：「情熱的な、熱烈な」
- **p.149 beautifully**：「見事に、美しく」
- **p.149 be flattered by ...**：「〜をうれしく思う」。多くの場合、自分のことをほめられたときの返事として、I'm flattered. または It's flattering. と言って気持ちを伝えます。

おわりに

A Final Word

Imagine it's evening. We're at a bar in Shibuya, sharing a bottle of scotch. The lights are low and soft music fills the air. You're probably wondering if the stories I've shared with you are true. Well, they are certainly based on true experiences-the many unforgettable experiences which have made my life in Japan so enjoyable.

Now, if you don't mind, I would like to share with you a little more about my life.

I was born in Argentina "some" years ago. After graduating in electronics, I came to Japan to attend Sophia University for one year. One year became two, and before I knew it, I had spent thirteen years working at a Japanese company.

Adapting to Japanese customs wasn't easy, so, for fun, I wrote stories about my experiences. I also wanted to show others that, from the right perspective, adapting to a different culture could be a great experience.

Sometimes, my stories caused problems. One evening, I finished a funny story about my boss and faxed it to my publisher before going to bed. When I arrived at my company the next day, my boss was already at his desk. "Fun," he said, "come here." As I approached his desk, my face turned red: he was holding the story I thought I had sent to the publisher! I had mistaken the fax number! "It's about a boss I had in

Argentina," I lied. He was mad and calmed down only after I offered to buy him a case of Argentine wine.

Although my native language is Spanish, I choose to write in English to show you that it's possible to learn and use a foreign language, even if your understanding of it isn't perfect. Remember, English is one of the main languages used throughout the world.

Now that I've shared my story, let's be friends. And now that we're friends, may I ask you a favor? Can you pay the bill? I've forgotten my wallet!

Fun Volga

著者紹介
Fun Volga（ファン・ボルガ）

1959年アルゼンチン生まれ。コルドバ・カトリック大学電子工学課卒。10才のころからブリティッシュアカデミーに通い、英語をマスター、国際人としての基礎を固める。1983年に初来日。上智大学大学院でマネジメントを学んだ後、日本の大手コンピュータ会社、銀行にて英語力を発揮し、海外マーケティングや国際ビジネスのマネジャーとして活躍する。通算在日年数は12年以上。

　エッセイストとしても英語系雑誌を中心に執筆活動を続け、自らが体験した様々なカルチャー・ギャップを「不思議の国ニッポン体験記」として、「English Zone」の前身誌である「Mini World」に連載。独特のユーモア感覚で愛すべき日本と日本人を描いた抱腹絶倒のストーリーは好評を博す。その連載をまとめたエッセイ集は本国で1992年アルゼンチン作家協会エッセイ賞を受賞した。

おもろすぎるわ日本人！

どーもどーも
パラダイス

"Domo Domo" Paradise

2003年3月6日　第1刷発行

著者　　　　　　ファン・ボルガ
イラストレーション　細馬一紀
デザイン　　　　　コウチデザイン
発行者　　杉本　惇
発行所　　（株）中経出版
〒102-0083　東京都千代田区麹町3-2　相互麹町第一ビル
電話　03-3262-8535（編集代表）　03-3264-2771（営業代表）
FAX　03-3262-6855　振替　00110-7-86836
ホームページ　　http://www.englishzone.jp/

DTP　エム・エー・ディー
印刷　三松堂印刷
製本　三森製本所

乱丁本・落丁本はお取替え致します。

Copyright © 2003 by Fun Volga, Printed in Japan.
ISBN 4-8061-1773-0 C2082

English Zone

中級以上を
めざすあなたの
英語メディア

全国書店で好評発売中!

奇数月1日発売
1月1日・3月1日・5月1日
7月1日・9月1日・11月1日

定価:本体1200円+税
B5判並製、96ページ

CD付

大好評の創刊号

表紙:
中級以上をめざすあなたの英語メディア
English Zone #001 創刊!
http://www.englishzone.jp

パワフル単独インタビュー集!
高野志穂
ジョン・カビラ
冨永愛
別所哲也
吉田兄弟
小柴昌俊
タフィ・ローズ
KONISHIKI
パトリック・ハーラン
トム・クルーズ
スティーブン・スピルバーグ

英語が私を強くする!
Think Aim High

「英語ができればいいのはわかってる、でもどれだけ頑張っても思うように伸びない……」、そんな思い、ありませんか。English Zoneは、面白いテーマを高校卒業レベルの英語で提供しながら、読者の皆さんをTOEIC® Test 730点レベル、さらにその上に導きます!

English Zone 3大特長

1 English Zoneの記事は「簡単な英語」で書かれている。だから読みやすい!

2 English Zoneの記事は全てオリジナル。「ここでしか読めないテーマ」を提供します。

3 理解度を確かめられる。読み続けられる。だからEnglish Zone。

English Zone 付録CD

リスニング&発音のスキルアップ!

本誌から選んだ記事をネイティブのプロ・ナレーターが音読します。各記事の後にはリスニング力がチェックできるQ&Aと発音練習に役立つPronunciation Cornerがついています。また、一部の記事は若干ゆっくり読まれています。

CD収録時間約70分

English Zone Web

http://www.englishzone.jp/

「英語の頭」に変わるサイト!英語をツールに楽しみながらステップアップできるコンテンツがいっぱい!

定期購読受付中! 7,560円(年6回配本、税込み・送料無料)

お問い合わせ先
(株)中経出版 English Zone 編集部
Tel:03-3262-8535 Fax:03-3262-6855 E-mail:ez@chukei.co.jp
http://www.englishzone.jp/

English Zone Books 第2弾 6月上旬刊行!

これであなたもアメリカ人(仮)

「朝のひととき」「ちょっと外食」など、日常にありがちなシチュエーションで、実際にもっとも使われる英会話表現を、マンガ形式で紹介。ゲストに、パックンマックンのパトリック・ハーランさんを迎えた、超実用的マンガ英会話本。全46話、対訳・注釈付き。

English Zone 奇数月1日発売

英語で楽しく読む。だから力になる。

English Zone #001
特集 インタビュー集
英語が私を強くする!

高野志穂／ジョン・カビラ
／冨永愛／別所哲也 ほか

English Zone #002
特集 英語で出会う
あなただけの愛のかたち

マイケル・J・フォックス／石川亜沙美
／リサ・ステッグマイヤー／倉田真由美 ほか